COUNSELING WITH PARENTS OF HANDICAPPED CHILDREN

Guidelines for Improving Communication

Elizabeth J. Webster, Ph.D.
Professor of Speech Pathology
Memphis State University
Speech and Hearing Center
Memphis, Tennessee

GRUNE & STRATTON
A Subsidiary of Harcourt Brace Jovanovich, Publishers
New York   San Francisco   London

362.7
Web

Library of Congress Cataloging in Publication Data

Webster, Elizabeth J
  Counseling with parents of handicapped children.

  Bibliography: p.
  Includes index.
  1. Handicapped children—Family relationships.
  2. Counseling. I. Title.
  HV888.W4   362.7'8'4   77-22098
  ISBN 0-8089-1036-1

Grune & Stratton, Inc.
111 Fifth Avenue
New York, New York   10003

Distributed in the United Kingdom by
Academic Press, Inc. (London) Ltd.
24/28 Oval Road, London NW 1

Library of Congress Catalog Number 77–22098
International Standard Book Number 0-8089-1036–1

Printed in the United States of America

For the many remarkable people who have meant so much to me, including my own parents and extended family, I am grateful to have met you in this life.

Contents

ACKNOWLEDGMENTS

Gratitude is extended to the following for permission to quote from published works: Excerpts from pages XII and 155 in *The Helping Interview*, Second Edition, by Alfred Benjamin, Copyright 1974 by the Houghton Mifflin Company; "Sovereignty" and an excerpt from "Rainbows" by James Dillet Freeman in *Daily Word*, copyright 1975 by Unity; an excerpt from "Parents of Children with Communication Disorders" by Elizabeth J. Webster, appearing in *Communication Disorders: An Appraisal*, edited by Alan J. Weston, copyright 1972 by Charles C. Thomas.

FOREWORD

People who are reading the foreword of a book on parent counseling don't need to be told that parent counseling is important—they are already demonstrating an interest. Yet it does seem important to point out that educators and other professionals, speech pathologists and audiologists, psychologists, etc., have expressed considerable ambivalence over the years about whether their work with a given child or a given client should be defined to include direct work with parents. Within this basic ambivalence there has also been a variety of responses from those who felt as though contact between parent and professional was important. Some have defined this contact as an educational experience, some as a psychotherapeutic process, and there have been a variety of points in between these poles.

In responding to this book it might be useful to have some sense of where the author has been on the way to this effort. More than 20 years ago, Betty Webster was one of a small group of people, primarily located at the University of Alabama, who were exploring a number of frontiers in the interpersonal relationship frequently known as speech therapy. In describing professional work with individuals with speech and hearing disorders as an interpersonal relationship, I reflect the basic orientation of the author, that is, that education, speech and hearing services, and other related ventures are not totally understood if looked upon solely as a sequence of activities, a body of information, or a series of tasks. Instead one must look first to the relationship between the persons involved as a way of defining what will go on within that relationship. In addition to exploring this richer philosophical and theoretical basis for speech therapy, Webster was instrumental in developing group therapy with speech-impaired individuals and in refining the use of psychotherapeutic tools such as counseling and roleplaying in the treatment of speech and hearing disorders. She was one of those interested in broadening the theoretical underpinnings of speech therapy to include writings in psychology, psychiatry, philosophy, language, and religion into a broad humanistic pattern. Many of the ideas that she and her colleague Louise Ward explored under the leadership of Ollie Backus are now commonplace, but they were actively resisted and rejected in those early days.

In this book she calls on her experience as a professional who has worked on a firsthand basis with parents over the course of her professional career, and not as an ivory tower expert. Webster bridges the gap between education and psychotherapeutically oriented counseling. She writes of giving and receiving information. She writes of establishing a basic contract or understanding between the counselor and the parent. She discusses the mechanics of both beginning and terminating a series of sessions, and these specifics provide the structure within which the parent and counselor can have the freedom to explore feelings as well as facts. She believes that counseling should be conducted within an orientation that stresses the nature of messages both verbal and nonverbal, and which is determined by attitudes which form not only the counselor-parent but the parent–child relationship.

In recent years the Bureau of Education for the Handicapped has funded several hundred demonstration preschool programs. In these programs the role of the parent has been a key ingredient, and we have watched many parents grow from the passive recipients of information into dynamic participants in the process of educating their children and in planning and developing policy and programs. There is a new readiness to look again at parents and professionals and at how they interact. Despite this experience many professionals still tend to assume that the parents somehow lose their ability to be creative partners in a learning experience around the time a child ends his preschool years. Having read this book, absorbed its philosophy as well as its techniques, I think the reader will be unlikely to retreat from the significance of work with parents as part of the total professional task.

> *Ed Martin*
> Bureau of Education
>   for the Handicapped
> Washington, D. C.

PREFACE

It is not the year that is new;
The moments, always the same,
Run newborn and naked to you
To clothe them and give them a name.

And declare them new or old.
You are the moments' lord
And mind the master mold;
You reckon and record

The meaning of events;
Not time, but you decide.
The moments hasten hence
And vanish; you abide.

Not by time's casual chance,
But in eternity
You have significance
And are what you will be.

James Dillet Freeman

These words reflect much of what I feel is the essence of my work: After more than 20 years it is ever new. Each parent of a handicapped child is different, as is each member of that family, and each situation with them. Each encounter brings so many oppportunities, indeed, so many challenges, that can spur one to grow as a human being. Such enriching and thought-provoking encounters have led me, or prodded me, to continue my own self-development. I think one cannot attempt to listen to the worlds of parents, trying to catch a glimpse of the existential dilemmas they confront, the joys and sorrows they experience, and the creativity they possess, without being stirred to confront similar aspects of one's own existence. At least this has been true for me.

I have similar thoughts about the students with whom I interact in courses and workshops about counseling. Each encounter with students is new and challenging. Students, too, are at various stages of development arising from various backgrounds, experiences, and needs. Their questions, confusions, disappointments, and successes have prompted me to try to improve ways to guide them. As has been the case in relationships with parents, I also have found that when I try to participate in the lives of students I experience profound influences on my own life. Students have taught me some of my most important lessons.

Over the course of time I have realized that what I do with both parents and students is to participate in various situational forms of the phenomenon of people gathering together, to try to communicate productively and in this way to learn, to cope, and to develop as persons. I realize that all of us are beings in the process of becoming, starting from wherever we are, trying to state our questions, confusions, hopes, and joys. We are all beings daring to reveal our ignorances as well as our feelings of success, and hoping through the process of our interaction to become more than we were. To paraphrase James Dillet Freeman, we have significance and are what we will be.

A book can sometimes stimulate the development of both its author and its readers, and my overriding concern in preparing this one has been to participate with others who seek, as I do, to function more effectively in counseling. I think of this book as both basic text and resource because the ideas and activities will be new to some readers and very familiar to others.

This material was developed for classes, workshops, and conferences dealing with parents, and most of the examples are from parent interviews. However the issues, principles, and procedures are the same no matter whether one counsels a parent, spouse, or sibling of a person with a handicap. Therefore the ideas and information about parents can be applied to others in the milieu of handicapped persons.

The persons who helped to evolve these materials represented such professions as speech pathology and audiology; social work; and early childhood, elementary, and special education. Many of them were also parents. Others who used and evaluated the materials were nonprofessionally trained parents. All of these persons were most generous in helping to select those items that seemed most useful for increasing their confidence and sharpening their skills.

Although it contains numerous suggestions, this is in no way a recipe book. Because each counselor is a unique individual, the processes involved in learning to interact constructively and productively cannot be reduced to recipe form. Rather, the ideas and suggestions presented here should be construed as possibilities for helping individuals to build a unique and creative repertoire of skills.

Because I am convinced that a counselor's greatest resource is the ability to develop meaningful and productive communication, this skill area will be emphasized. Again, I have not visualized my task as producing a formula for instant success in communicating with parents because, while some of the ingredients of good communication are known, there is no set way to combine them to produce a skilled communicator. Rather, my hope is to help you, the reader, to become increasingly aware of the rich reservoir of communication skills you now possess. Your task is to acknowledge such communicative abilities, to broaden and deepen them, and to apply them in your work with parents. This, then, is a shared endeavor.

As we begin to explore ways to counsel effectively, we should agree on certain terms. *Parent* refers to one who serves as *caretaker* for a child. The person may be the natural parent or grandparent, aunt, uncle, and so forth. Or the person may have no blood relationship to the child, such as a foster parent. The important variable is that the person serve a caretaking function.

I have selected *counseling* rather than *training* or *education* to refer to work with parents because those who are involved with parents do not *merely* teach or train them. Counselors do not do any one thing with and for parents; they do many. The term *counseling* seems broad enough to embrace all the various functions served and thus does not limit role definition. Therefore I prefer to use *parent counseling* rather than such terms as *parent training* or *parent education,* which seem to limit conceptualization of counselors' roles. Specific functions served by counselors will be discussed in detail, because the functions are more crucial than the label by which they are designated.

There should also be agreement on what the term *counseling* does not mean as it is used here. This term is not used to refer only to the work of those who are psychotherapists. It is obvious that all who work with handicapped children, most of whom are not trained psychotherapists, will from time to time have to interact with the parents of those children. Thus workers will be confronted by both the cognitive and emotional dimensions of parents. They will recognize that parents need help not only with management, but also in understanding and clarifying their ideas, attitudes, and emotions. Furthermore, parents of handicapped children do not routinely seek psychotherapy (Heisler, 1972), but first tend to seek help for themselves from those who serve their children. Such workers can provide meaningful help in most cases. Those parents who can be identified as wanting or needing psychotherapy can be referred to those trained to give them such assistance in addition to the help provided through the types of experiences to be discussed here.

Although most persons who counsel parents are not psychotherapists, all of them provide therapeutic benefits to the extent that they try to meet parental needs. Any counselor–parent contact has the potential for therapeutic benefits for both parties. That is, any encounter has the potential to be a healing, rewarding, and constructive experience, rather than one that is unrewarding, destructive, or what Bates and Johnson (1972) called "toxic."

Just as parent–counselor interactions will be termed *counseling,* those who engage in helping parents will be called *counselors.* It should be pointed out that all those who are successful counselors need not have a professional speciality. Many nonprofessional persons are excellent counselors; for example, many parents of handicapped children have developed great skill in counseling with other parents. The contributions of nonprofessionals must be appreciated and encouraged, and it is hoped that the materials in this book will be useful to them.

For the term to designate parent–counselor interactions, I have used *session, meeting,* or *interview* as they were used by Benjamin (1974). These terms are used interchangeably.

There is, however, a major problem with the English language. It has no term for both *he* and *she,* and I refuse to refer to anyone as *it.* Therefore, when the singular pronoun seems essential, *he* will be used for the sake of brevity and with full acknowledgment that a great many counselors and one-half the parents of the world are women.

Another problem is that of assessing the outcomes of counseling. There are still serious limitations on knowledge about parents of handicapped children, about their needs, and about how best to help

them. These areas of ignorance make it extremely difficult to evaluate the results of counseling efforts. For example, although parents
may report feeling better about themselves and their children following parent counseling, they may not reveal dramatic behavioral
changes. However, as I stated earlier (1972, p. 365), "the needs of
parents are impelling; they cannot wait for further studies [of the
outcomes of counseling]. Counselors must work from available
knowledge. They must also work from a value system in which they
attempt to assist children, to assist their parents, and to damage
neither in the process."

In view of limited knowledge, counselors should be careful not
to overgeneralize about the right or the wrong thing to do with
parents, and I have tried to exercise such caution. This is not to say
that counselors should avoid developing logical rationales for what
they do. Rather, each counselor must develop a rationale that is
consistent with known principles and facts, while humbly recognizing that all the principles are not yet known and that all the facts are
not yet in.

It should be noted that models for parent counseling vary
greatly because of the preferences of the people involved and because of situational differences. Some professionals work with both
children and their parents (as is usually the case with classroom
teachers), whereas other professionals work only with parents (as is
the case when I work with parents during the time that their children
receive therapy.) Variations in counseling models also occur because of variations in frequency and length of contacts; for example, a pediatrician sees parents less often and probably for shorter
visits than does the child's classroom teacher. Finally, the purpose
of contacts with parents varies, ranging from giving information to
helping a parent change behavior.

In spite of variation in counseling models, it is a misconception
to think that frequency, length, or purpose of contacts with parents
should determine counselor behavior. Rather, counselors should
select the principles on which they will operate and apply these in all
their contacts with parents; they need not seek unique principles to
apply to unique situations.

Although principles do not vary from one situation to another,
procedures should be varied systematically with the frequency,
length, and purpose of each parent contact. A number of procedures
will be discussed and some of the potential pitfalls in each will be

pointed out. The procedures that seem more useful when meeting with several parents for repeated visits rather than for only one or two interviews, will be noted.

In planning this book I have worked on the assumption that those who work with parents need information about them and explanations of counseling principles. More importantly, counselors need to be helped to tap the wellsprings of their own creativity. Each person has an inner reservoir of creativity, and I hope that this book will help counselors to get in touch with their own creative potential, to acknowledge and build their own unique ways of perceiving and responding, and to experiment freely with various procedures. I have conceived of your task as reader to be that of experimenting freely with behaviors stemming from the principles discussed here; you should also continue experimentation long enough to arrive at an adequate assessment of the extent to which use of these principles enables you to communicate more creatively and constructively.

The first step is to get in touch with and clarify your attitudes about yourself and others. This is not busywork. Attitudes inevitably will be communicated in behavior, so it is important that they be sorted out and understood.

Clarification of one's assumptive world is a process that lasts a lifetime. At the same time that one is engaged in this process, one can also experiment with various ways of behaving with parents. It is my hope that these ideas and suggestions will assist you in both aspects of your experimentation.

People seem most free to experiment with attitudes and behaviors in an atmosphere that is relatively safe and free from threat, and where reward is received for relatively successful performance. The key to learning seems to be to build on small successes: People need to have some things that turn out well. You should keep this in mind as you work with the practice exercises in this book, some of which I designed for groups and some of which can be done by one person working alone. It will probably be easier to receive positive reinforcement when you work along with others; if you work alone, please attend carefully to your performance and praise yourself for success.

As you read the examples of counselor and parent statements, please note that these came from tape recordings or notes of actual interviews. Clients' and counselors' names have of course been changed; it is obvious that hardly anyone really has the name Mrs. A. In some cases the grammar has been changed slightly, but the examples are of real people expressing real ideas and emotions.

In sharing ideas and experiences in written form, I realize that there are two serious limitations. There is the limitation imposed by the printed word. Words in print are one-dimensional; they lose the richness of spoken language, in which factors such as intonation and rate play a vital role in imparting meaning. Because words used in written examples seem flat and devoid of life, they are subject to misunderstanding. I suggest that you read the examples aloud so that you can hear how they might sound when spoken. Another limitation is imposed by the fact that I do not have your direct and immediate feedback, and therefore I have no chance to consider your questions and to further explain my thoughts or to sharpen them.

These are very real limitations. Nevertheless, I hope this book can serve as a source of reinforcement for the counseling skills you now possess and for your attempts to further refine your ideas and skills in this area.

As we explore the topic of parent counseling, I wish to acknowledge further the help I have received. I continue to feel deeply grateful for my long-time good friends Louise M. Ward and Ollie Backus, and the way each has influenced my thinking. Other influential persons include Zelda H. Kosh, Millie Almy, A. T. Jersild, and the many scholars, teachers, and clinicians whose work is referred to in subsequent pages. Edwin W. Martin's Foreword is gratefully acknowledged, as are his friendship and his efforts on behalf of many individuals in his role as Associate Deputy Commissioner of the Bureau of Education for the Handicapped. The delightful and informative critique of the manuscript provided by Janice Ward Parrish was invaluable, as were the comments of Marilyn Newhoff and Karen Folger. Finally, one who types as badly as I do can appreciate the patience and skill of Shirley Rias, Regina Cook, and Marcia Foncannon.

PART I

Parent Counseling as Interpersonal Communication

*As counselors consider their work with parents of children
with handicaps, they should remember that counseling is not
something one does* to *another person; it is an activity one does* with
*another. Counseling is an endeavor that people engage in together.
The term* counseling *is a very broad one, but it simply refers to a
number of situations in which people communicate. The same laws
that govern all interpersonal communication dictate what transpires
between counselors and parents. Counselor–parent communication
is subject to the various pitfalls that beset any communicative
endeavor, and it is more satisfying and productive at some times
than at others. Perhaps it is useful to think of counseling situations
as somewhat special interpersonal events because at least one
person, the counselor, attempts to communicate therapeutically and
constructively during these encounters.*

*Parent counseling usually involves at least two people in a face-
to-face encounter, although it can include such extensions as
telephone conversations or written messages. The principles of
counseling are the same whether one or several people are involved,
and no matter what channel is used to transmit messages. However
the model to be described in this book is face-to-face interaction,
because that is the most frequent model and it can be used to*

exemplify the principles governing all other types of parent–counselor interactions.

In the writer's view the first requisite for effective counseling is understanding and respect for the incredible complexity of human communication. It is also necessary to understand that it is not only parents whose communication is complicated. Counselors, too, are complex individuals whose communication will reflect their unique individual differences. In this section certain variables that are part of the human condition, and thus common to both counselors and parents, will be discussed. Counselors must understand these similarities as well as the uniquenesses of individuals as they consider their communication with parents.

1

Counselors and Parents are Similar as well as Different

PERCEPTION

Each person's communication depends first on perception, that is, how one receives the world. One can communicate only about one's perceptions of events, objects, and people. Perception, then, is considered the cornerstone in the foundation of communication. Each person's sensory receptors provide data from the outside world, making possible a certain amount of consistency in human perception. Nevertheless, there are numerous reasons for great individual variation in perceptual ability besides the obvious one of variation in sensory acuity. Forces that arise from within each person interface with external forces and exert such a powerful influence on perceptual abilities that no one can perceive any bit of data in precisely the same way. Because perception is so highly individualized, it seems imperative to examine some of the complexities introduced into it by the interplay of external and internal forces that arise from each person's experiences, associations, and needs.

Each person exists in a unique and very private world made up of forces that constantly impinge from both inside and outside. The outer forces help to create and shape one's inner world, while internal forces help to create and shape one's perception of the outer world.

3

Each person's private world is also in a state of continuous change because of constant and instantaneous changes in either inner or outer forces, or both. One need only think of one's biologic makeup to find many examples of such continual change and to recognize that while some changes take place rapidly, others come about more slowly. Another example can be found in how the words on this page came to be as they are. In order for these words to be written, thoughts (inner forces) had to produce them; after the words were produced, they became the outer forces that served to stir such additional internal stimuli as more thoughts, attitudes, questions, or meanings.

One can be aware of many of these internal stimuli and quite unaware of others. For example, a man accustomed to eating lunch promptly at noon every day may experience difficulty in paying close attention to the last part of a class or meeting that extends to 12:45 because inner forces of hunger prompt awareness of the need for lunch. The man may be unaware of these forces and may wonder why he is increasingly restless.

Such internal stimuli, whether or not the person is aware of them, govern the ability to abstract from, to understand, and to interpret external events. Thus internal stimuli can be seen to exert great control over the type and amount of data that one can perceive and process at any one time.

The influence of coexisting internal and external forces also results in the fact that a person's perception will always be fragmented. One has no choice but to be selective; that is, because of internal forces one will be aware of certain aspects of the outer world and quite unaware of other aspects. Likewise, one will sometimes be aware of certain aspects of the outer world that will escape notice at other times. To return to the above example of the writing of words, and given that there is an infinite number of word combinations in which to clothe thoughts, the writer can be aware of some of her options, but in no case is it possible to be aware of all of them; certain word choices will come to mind at one time that would not have come into awareness at other times. The old story of the seven blind men touching different parts of an elephant with the result that each had a different conception of *elephant* illustrates this point (Keyes, 1963). All persons will have perceptual blind spots as they are bombarded by both internal and external forces, and these blind spots will change frequently.

The fact that internal stimuli interface with those from the external world to exert such power over perception has important ramifications for counselor-parent communication. The following implications will be mentioned here and elaborated in later chapters.

1. Counselors and parents can discuss only those matters perceived and processed into the awareness of each of them. Thus a parent will mention many items that the counselor will overlook, or only later think were important. Conversely, a counselor may start to discuss a certain topic only to be greeted by parental silence, not because the parent is stupid or resistant but because the parent simply does not perceive the topic as important at that time.

2. Neither counselors nor parents can modify any behavior unless they become aware that the behavior exists. For example, a counselor may be unaware of such behaviors as talking too much or too fast; only when the counselor becomes aware of the details of such behaviors can they be changed.

3. Counselors can serve parents by helping them to enlarge the amount of data they can perceive; that is, parents can be helped to notice, process, and use greater numbers of details.

4. It is important that counselors attempt to enlarge their own perceptual worlds and learn to use more differentiated perception if they wish to help parents to do the same. Counselors have long recognized the importance of working on various aspects of their own behavior if they are to help others (Rogers, 1951 chap. 3), and the same is true in learning to perceive in a more differentiated fashion.

PROJECTION

Projection is another factor present in all human beings. Readers who have thought of projection only as an aspect of psychopathology need to enlarge their thinking to recognize this phenomenon in all functioning persons. The human mind has the ability to form images or impressions, or to come to conclusions. These internal impressions or conclusions are then directed outward; that is, they are projected onto persons, objects, and events in the outer world. In this way one's projections shape one's outer reality.

Because projection determines so much of the view one has of the outer world, its influence on communication is obvious. To state this fact in a highly oversimplified way, one projects what one expects to perceive and then proceeds to perceive that which will support this conception; one imagines what one will find in the outer world, sets out to find it, and sometimes does find it. Numerous examples come to mind. Perhaps you have had the experience of thinking a person was likely to be angry about something you did; when in a subsequent meeting the person was friendly, you may have been suspicious that the person was covering up hostility, or you may have hunted for signs of the anger you felt *certain* that the person felt. Or perhaps on first meeting a person you were aware of certain characteristics that reminded you of someone you liked very much, and you felt immediately drawn to the newcomer. Conversely, your projected impressions can lead you to stand back warily from a person, even on a first meeting.

People communicate with the images that they project. People also communicate about their projections. The importance of these facts should not be overlooked in parent counseling. A parent will talk with the *projected image* of the counselor. Many counselors have had the experience of hearing parents refer to such projected images. For example, one mother made a very succinct statement about the influence of projection when she said as she left her first session with me, "Well, you weren't as hard to talk to as I thought you were going to be." Another mother was speaking of projection when she said, "No one will ever know how hard it was for me to drag myself here the first time. I thought we'd talk about all the things I've done wrong with Mike." Lest the reader think projections can only be negative, it was also a projected image that was reflected by a father who said, "Anthony's teacher has got to be the soul of patience to be so good with him."

Counselors also respond to parents who are in large part projected images. To illustrate projection and its potential effects, I ask a student beginning my parent counseling course to write her impressions of parents immediately after meeting with them for the first time. Later, after their sixth meeting, students are again asked to write their impressions of the same parents, and it is interesting to note that many of their first impressions have changed. Incidentally, there is nothing magic about a 6-week acquaintance if one wishes to clarify one's original projections; this exercise only illustrates the presence of projections, how they influence counselor communication, and how projections can be clarified and modified.

It should be noted that some projections seem quite open to the influence of new data and thus are relatively easily changed, while others seem almost impervious to change. There are many examples of such stubborn projections: the ability to see good in a person you know has been dishonest with you or has talked against you; the parts of your long-time friendships that are your projections of positive attributes of the friends; or your inability to think of a person as attractive even though other people are enthusiastic about the person.

That people tend to respond to their projected images is not abnormal. It is human. However the tendency to project results in the likelihood that a person will equate what is inside his own head with what is outside; that is, one may be convinced that one's own projections and resultant perceptions are what is true and right. Of course one's projected images are not necessarily true; indeed, they may not even be shared by other persons. It is even more dangerous when one insists that other people agree with one's projected images. Such insistence almost inevitably leads to unsatisfying and unproductive communication, because no two people can possibly project images that are exactly alike.

Counselors need to understand and accept the fact that as an outgrowth of the human situation, no two people will view the world in precisely the same way; each will abstract only those details he can perceive at the moment. Further, reality changes rapidly for every person. Each person also projects different images at different times. For all of these reasons, counselors and parents are likely to disagree. However counselors can recognize that it is very fortunate that there are individual variations in perception and projection. Because of these differences, counselors can experience the satisfaction of discussing, expanding, and sharpening their perceptual worlds through interaction with parents.

Counselors can also be grateful that they share common bonds with parents in matters of projection and perception, because this sharing makes each of them much more simply human than otherwise, to use Sullivan's terms (Mullahy, 1952). Counselors can feel comfortable in the knowledge that all parties involved in parent counseling share the same human frailities and thus all have similar limitations.

DESIRE FOR GROWTH AND CHANGE

Another shared aspect of humanness is that both parents and counselors desire to change, to become better than they are now. Because counselors can perceive themselves as beings who want to change and develop, they are more likely to see parents in the same light. To this writer, the counselor's awareness of the human desire for growth serves as the basis for respectful and productive communication. Further, as counselors pursue their acquaintance both with themselves and with parents, they will learn about the great strength, courage, stamina, and resiliency that are also aspects of being human.

It cannot be stated too strongly that it is essential to understand these influences on one's communication, and on that of others, if a counselor is to communicate constructively, because such understanding leads to respect for self and others. Respect, in turn, leads a counselor to try to create an atmosphere in which parents can feel trust, to grant parents freedom to grow and change as persons in their own right (and not just because they should change to help their children), and to provide opportunities for parents to experiment and feel successful. Murphy (1976) pointed out the unique opportunities parent counseling provides for both parents and counselors to develop greater humanness through their interactions.

REACTIONS TO CRISIS

Another similarity between counselors and parents is the fact that all human beings experience dramatic reactions to crisis, however delayed those reactions may be. An example familiar to most car drivers is that of remaining cool and collected just long enough to narrowly avoid an accident, and a split second later beginning to shake, or having a horrible sinking feeling in the pit of the stomach, or feeling extreme anger, or engaging in some individual version of a total and dramatic reaction to that particular crisis. The situations that individuals perceive as crises vary of course, but no one escapes the experience of crisis.

It is possible that parents of a handicapped child may experience more crises than many other people, the first one occurring when they discover that something is wrong with the child. In the experience of this writer and others (Brutten, Richardson, & Mangel, 1973), parents of a seriously impaired child often know that something is wrong with their child long before a professional diagnostician specifically describes the problem; so for these parents crisis can extend over a long period of time. Furthermore, such continuing parental tasks as caring for the child, providing treatment or education, coping with financial strains, or providing for other family members, can create continuing parental crises.

Shontz (1965) has postulated that there may be four stages of reaction to crises: shock, realization, defensive retreat, and acknowledgment. Examples of how these stages might occur in the parents of a handicapped child will be given in Chapter 4. The important points to remember here are that because counselors have experienced crises, they should be able to better understand parental crises, that counselor–parent communication may take place in the midst of a crisis, and that a reaction to crisis may serve as the topic of counselor–parent discussion.

It is also important to remember that the very act of talking with a counselor can stir parental awareness of factors previously outside of awareness; thus the discussion itself can create a situation in which parents experience crisis. When a counselor is aware that a parent is experiencing a crisis, it could lead to counselor compassion rather than rejection. For example, the counselor might wonder, "What is this crisis like for this mother?" rather than wondering, "Why is she so stubborn?" or thinking, "She's a weird one," or having some such negative reaction.

Counselors have the opportunity to help parents toward resolution of their crises. Through discussion, counselors can help parents communicate about, clarify, and cope with their reactions to what they perceive as critical situations. More will be said about helping with the process of clarification in chapter 10.

SUMMARY

Each person's reality has been referred to as a private world because it is formed by, and is exclusive to, that person. It seems important that counselors understand this privacy. They cannot fully know and understand any parent, just as any parent cannot fully know and understand a counselor.

Because of this and other factors mentioned in this chapter, it is inevitable that as counselors and parents interact, there will be vast individual differences between them. It is equally important to understand that counselors and parents will have numerous similarities. They will share the commonalities inherent in living and communicating as human beings. They will also share the desire to receive something from their time together; that is, each person will seek to have the counseling encounters contribute to further self-development. Each party in the counseling situation has experienced, and will experience, crises. It is hoped, however, that through the process of discussion, each can be helped to clarify and cope with crisis situations.

STUDY GUIDES FOR CHAPTER 1

Additional Readings

Keyes, K. S. *How to improve your thinking ability.* (Paperback Ed.). New York: McGraw-Hill, 1963, Parts I and II.

Murphy, A. Parent counseling and exceptionality: From creative insecurity to increased humanness. In E. Webster (Ed.), *Professional approaches with parents of handicapped children.* Springfield: Charles C. Thomas, 1976, pp. 3–26.

Patton, B. & Giffin, K. *Interpersonal communication: Basic text and readings.* New York: Harper & Row, 1974, pp. 156–212.

Practice Exercises

1. To illustrate differences in the way people perceive the outer world, observe an object and write a description of the first five details of

which you are aware. Comparison of your descriptions with those of others will illustrate differences in perception of details. Observing the object again later will illustrate that you are aware of different details at different times. This exercise can be repeated with observations of people and/or events.

2. This exercise requires a considerable amount of honest communication with yourself. Think about someone whom you like very much and describe several attributes of that person that are to some degree your own projected images. Then think of someone to whom you usually have a negative reaction. What attributes do you find in that person that you don't like in yourself? Question yourself about the extent to which you may be projecting an image.

2

Understanding the Nature
of Messages

Whenever people interact, they inevitably communicate with each other. Authors such as Stent (1972) contend that all living things communicate, and it is probable that human beings cannot keep from communicating. Human beings have the power to communicate both verbally and nonverbally, and counselors should recognize the importance of both verbal and silent messages.

While the basic design of communication is simple, consisting of a message sender and a receiver who processes and interprets the message before sending a return message, the seeming simplicity of the process is misleading. In order to be perceived and processed, messages must stir internal forces. Barnlund (1971) pointed out that messages create the meanings within the receiver that interprets the message. Thus, counselors' and parents' messages contain content (the topic) and meaning (that which one intends to convey and that which is understood by the receiver of the message). In Chapter 1 it was stated that because of the influence of projection on perception, it is possible for a counselor's message to generate meanings that are quite different from those the counselor intended. Counselors seem to recognize that the content of messages is vitally important. Content should be delivered in language that is understandable. It also helps if content is stated succinctly.

Furthermore, because the meanings of messages are even more

important than their contents (Barnlund, 1971), the content of a message should be congruent with, or true to, the intended meaning of its sender. For example, "I am *so* angry" is a congruent message from one who is very angry, and "I am *delighted*" is congruent with feelings of pleasure, joy, and delight. Conversely, incongruent messages are those in which content is not true to the sender's internal meanings. For example, "It was a pleasure to see you" is an incongruent message when its sender was bored in the presence of the one addressed.

Congruent communication is no simple task. Taking into account the complexities inherent in the persons who are counselors and parents, it is little wonder that it is difficult for either of them to send congruent messages. Language is inadequate for expressing many ideas and emotions. Furthermore, each person operates at any time with perceptions that are distorted by projection, and each may be unaware of the internal meanings prompting a message. The basic sender–receiver model is an intricate interplay of forces that promote communication and those that impede it. The complexity of the model, and thus of the web of forces, increases dramatically when more than two people meet together. Further complications in message sending and receiving arise from the additional factors discussed below.

Each communicative act is irrepeatable; that is to say, each act of communication creates its own meanings, to which responses are made, and the process for the communicative act is then over. Each communicative act can be compared to a strain of music that is played, experienced at the moment, then ended.

Communication is a circular, forward-moving process. When one person communicates, another person must respond; there is no way to prevent response. Each response is a communicative act that prompts some kind of response, either spoken or unspoken, in return. This circular process is irreversible. Every person probably has experienced this phenomenon of irreversibility. Everyone has at some time said angry words and immediately wished to take them back, but one cannot "un-say" words. One can, however, amend a message. In the case of regretted angry words, one can diminish the negative meanings possibly created in the receiver by sending another message.

It is fortunate for productive communication that there often are opportunities for amending messages and thus opening the door for possible additional or corrected interpretations. An example from a recorded conversation between two women in a parent group may illustrate how a message is irreversible but still possible to amend. Mrs. A. was discussing how angry she felt when other adults stared at her 4-year-old son, who was very tiny and wore thick glasses and a hearing aid. The conversation proceeded as follows.

MRS. A: I just want to scream at those people. I want to yell, "I'm so mad, I could beat on you! Where are your manners!" My husband says to just ignore them like he does. In fact, he doesn't even seem to notice.

MRS. B: Boy, I'm glad my husband doesn't withdraw like that! I need his help.

MRS. A: Oh no, George [her husband] doesn't withdraw.

MRS. B: But you say he ignores those people.

MRS. A: Well, yes, he does, but he's really a friendly type. Those people just don't seem to make him mad like they do me.

MRS. B: Oh, you mean he's more even-tempered than you are.

MRS. A: Right, now you've got it, he sure is. I'm the high-strung worrier in the family.

It can be seen that the meanings of messages are influenced by the total personality, background, and experience of both sender and receiver. Just as messages cannot be separated from either their sender or receiver, neither can sender or receiver discard a total personality comprised of needs, associations, experiences, and values in order to send a message. Each person brings all aspects of self —intelligence, ideas, self-concept, trust, expectancies, and goals— into each communicative act. The inevitable total participation of each person increases both the complexity of communication and its potential productivity.

NONVERBAL COMMUNICATION

The matter of silent communication deserves further attention. Any message contains powerful nonverbal elements. Potent message carriers include changes in facial expression, shrugging the shoulders or waving the hands, or the total bodily response of moving toward or away from another person during conversation. Because these nonverbal communications are so vital to meaning, often more important than verbal elements, they deserve special counselor consideration.

Mehrabian (1972) is among those who have pointed out that when verbal and nonverbal aspects of a message are congruent, the message-sender's meaning is likely to be perceived and understood as intended, making productive communication possible. However, communication is distorted and confusing, and thus potentially unproductive, if verbal and nonverbal messages are perceived as incongruent. In fact, when verbal and nonverbal elements are incongruent, the nonverbal aspects may have the more potent influence on the meaning given to a message (Argyle, 1975; Mehrabian, 1969; Strahan & Zytowski, 1976).

Incongruous messages are confusing because garbled content and meanings must be sorted out by the receiver. Incongruities can also introduce conflict. There are many examples of such conflicting responses. Perhaps you don't know how to respond to a woman who says, "I'm so glad to see you again," while looking as if she can't remember either your name or where she may have seen you. Or perhaps you don't know how to respond to a person who says how much he is enjoying your company while at the same time hunting for the nearest exit. Have you wondered what to say to a person proclaiming, "I'm not worried," or "I'm not really nervous," while sitting forward in a chair with a tense face, perhaps also biting his nails and showing other signs of tension?

The need to sort these garbled messages or to handle the conflicts they introduce can lead to listener resentment. Resentment also can be stirred when such incongruities lead the listener to perceive the message-sender as insincere or untrustworthy. It is precisely because people become confused and resentful by the incongruous messages they are given that this writer encourages counselors to examine not only their verbal communication but also the nonverbal elements of their messages.

SORTING THE USES OF LANGUAGE

Returning to the matter of verbal aspects of communication, the writer stated that counselors' spoken messages should convey their intended meanings as accurately as possible. This endeavor will be assisted if counselors will clarify three forms of language. These language forms are description, inference, and evaluation. When counselors confuse the three forms, they not only reflect confusion in their thinking but also are highly likely to bewilder listeners.

Description

Description is the clothing for one's observations. Observations are made by using one's sensory apparatus to receive stimuli. One can observe with the sensory mechanism unaided: one watches, listens, touches, smells, or tastes, and thus perceives. One also can observe with the senses aided by some other device. For example, one can aid one's vision by looking through a microscope, or one can hear more and different sounds by listening with a stethoscope, and so on.

If the senses are aided they may yield more data, or they may yield only different data. For example, a microscope is extremely helpful in analyzing a person's blood chemistry, but it cannot observe how that person sits in a chair. Again, a child's performance on a reading test can be observed by computing a score, but that score will neither reveal how the child approached the task, nor note his changes in facial expression during testing. Only the human observer—in this case, the tester—can observe these variables.

Observation with the senses, either aided or unaided, is the basis for description. Descriptive language is used to tell about observations. In other words, descriptive language tells about sensory data. The following very brief example of the description of a person will be used for illustration. One might report unaided sensory observations as: "A woman about 5 feet, 6 inches tall, weighing about 117 pounds, with blue eyes and blond hair, is wearing a blue dress and sandals. She is sitting at a desk with papers in front of her, holding a pencil in her right hand. Her head is bent forward, and her eyebrows are slightly drawn together."

Inference

The second language form is inference. Inference is used when one has collected enough observations to enable one to discover patterns in the data. By increasing the number of observations one makes, one increases the likelihood of a more accurate inference. But even with a large amount of data, an inference may not be entirely accurate. Therefore inferences are indexed as rather tentative statements, with qualifying words that allow for error. Returning to the above example to illustrate the use of inferences, note the use of such qualifiers as *seems, appears, is thought to be, may be,* or the use of the original description, to support an inference: "The woman is right-handed, and from the way she is sitting she appears to be concentrating on something she is writing. She may be a teacher working at the desk in her classroom. She seems well and appropriately dressed, and to judge from her sandals, the weather probably is warm. Her frown seems to indicate her deep concentration or to reveal that she is worried."

Evaluation

The third language form is evaluation. This is the form that most reflects judgments or conclusions. The person using evaluation may refer to an observed phenomenon only long enough to make a judgment about it; that is, description may be ignored in the process of judging, or it may be alluded to only to support the evaluation. Thus evaluation or judgment, in contrast to description, tells more about one's inner reaction to outer phenomena than it tells about the phenomena themselves. To state this another way, evaluative statements tell about what is going on inside the head of the person making the evaluation. Evaluations can be positive or negative statements because they refer to the speaker's values; such statements will reveal what the speaker considers right or wrong, worthy or unworthy, beautiful or ugly, and so forth.

Using the example of the woman at the desk one more time, note the absence of many references to descriptive information in the following evaluative statements: "She really looks like she hates her work. She's a pretty woman but she's so tense. Her dress isn't very pretty and it isn't becoming to her. She's smart to dress in light clothes in hot weather. She should get away from that desk and get outside more; she looks pale and some sun would help her pallor."

The understanding of evaluative statements involves considerable guesswork on the part of the listener who is trying to translate the message in order to understand the values being expressed. The following examples of counselors' evaluative statements are accompanied by possible translations to show how such statements tell more about the speaker's reactions than about the parent named in each example.

Evaluative Statement	*Possible Translation*
1. Mr. Jones is a cooperative father.	Mr. Jones has done what I wanted him to do.
2. He is such a handsome man.	I like the way he looks.
3. He's so virile.	I like the way he looks.
4. He has made excellent progress.	He has changed in ways that I value.
5. Mrs. Jones just isn't motivated.	I'm displeased that Mrs. Jones hasn't done what I asked her to do.
6. Johnny won't improve unless Mrs. Jones does.	Mrs. Jones is threatening my feeling of being skillful.

The above evaluative statements do not give information. They do not reveal such facts as how the parent looked, what the parent said, or what the parent did. While each statement probably has some basis in describable matters, nonetheless, in each the speaker states a reaction (in terms of speaker values) rather than describing external data.

Just as there are certain qualifying words, such as *seems* or *appears,* that signal that one is making an inference, there also are word clues that lead one to recognize evaluation. The use of various forms of the verb *to be* is one such clue. Adjectives also are used in evaluations. More subtle clues are such words as *always, never,* and *should* or *must.*

Gibb (1971) pointed out that when one makes evaluative statements one may increase the defensiveness of the other person. Particularly in the face of negative evaluation, the listener may immediately defend against the onslaught of such judgment. While there is an important place for evaluation in work with parents, and more will be said about this later, counselors should use evaluation with great caution.

To summarize this section dealing with three forms of language, it is thought particularly important that counselors not confuse both themselves and parents by failing to understand the differences in description, inference, and evaluation. Descriptions report data. Carefully made inferences provide information about how one has patterned the data and about the hypotheses one has made about the data. Evaluations may obscure information because they tell primarily about one's values and judgments. Counselors should also understand that each language form will be received differently by parents. The appropriate use of language is so crucial to effective counseling that counselors should spend whatever time is necessary to learn how and when to use each form. Each is useful, but they are different and useful for different purposes. The writer believes that counselors will need the most practice in becoming skillful users of description and inference; human beings have the marvelous ability to make judgments, and therefore do not seem to need extra practice in this area.

SUMMARY

It is erroneous to think of message sending and receiving as a simple process. Messages are sent for various reasons. They also are received with the various meanings a receiver attaches to them. Messages can be sent nonverbally, and verbal messages have important nonverbal elements influencing how the listener responds. Further communicative complications are introduced by the facts that the sending and receiving of messages is a circular and forward-moving process, that each communicative act is irrepeatable, and that description, inference, and evaluation are likely to be received differently.

STUDY GUIDES FOR CHAPTER 2

Additional Readings

Argyle, M. The syntaxes of bodily communication. In J. Benthall & T. Polhemus (Eds.), *The body as a medium of expression.* New York: E. P. Dutton, 1975, pp. 143–161.

Barnlund, D. Toward a meaning-centered philosophy of communication. In K. Giffin & B. Patton (Eds.), *Basic readings in interpersonal communication.* New York: Harper & Row, 1971, pp. 198–202.

Gibb, J. Defensive communication. In K. Giffin & B. Patton (Eds.), *Basic readings in interpersonal communication.* New York: Harper & Row, 1971, pp. 366–374.

Mehrabian, A. Some subtleties of communication. *Language, Speech and Hearing Services in Schools,* 1972, *3,* 62–67.

Mehrabian, A. Significance of posture and position in the communication of attitude and status relationships. *Psychological Bulletin,* 1969, *71,* 359–372.

Strahan, C., & Zytowski, D. Impact of visual, vocal, and lexical cues on judgments of counselor qualities. *Journal of Counseling Psychology,* 1976, *23,* 387–393.

Practice Exercises

1. As a way of becoming increasingly conscious of how messages create different meanings in different people, recall several messages that you heard differently from what another person said he heard. Note whether you thought the verbal or nonverbal elements of the message made the difference to you.

2. Mark each of the following statements as Descriptive (D), Inferential (I), or Evaluative (E). The author's choices are in Appendix A.

    ——a. John's grandmother brought him to the Reading Center.
    ——b. When Lila's mother came to school today, Lila appeared very upset.
    ——c. John's IQ on the Stanford-Binet is 89; his performance scores are consistently higher than his verbal scores.
    ——d. The Graduate Record Examination wasn't too hard.
    ——e. "You'll like him; he's such a cute kid."
    ——f. Steve's mother stated that he is 6 years old now.
    ——g. Steve is a stubborn boy.
    ——h. Mrs. Brown seems to feel tired very often.
    —— i. Mrs. Brown should feel tired with six children to manage.
    —— j. She really is a huge part of her son's problems.
    ——k. There were four people in the group today.
    —— l. It appears that the people in this group are acquainted with each other now because they seem talkative.

3

Understanding Important Counselor Attitudes

Even the brief consideration given here to the complex variables that govern communication leads to the conclusion that counselor attitudes are of utmost importance in work with parents. Counselors have long recognized (Rogers, 1951, chap. 3) that their attitudes about themselves and others, and about their counseling role, determine the satisfaction and productivity they and their clients experience. Counselors' attitudes also determine whether or not a client chooses to continue the counseling relationship. This is the primary reason counselors need to examine their attitudes, clarify them, and give immediate attention to those that seem to prevent constructive communication.

SELF-AWARENESS AND SELF-ACCEPTANCE

One is free to choose many of the attitudes with which one operates, and self-awareness seems to be the first step to greater self-acceptance as well as to modification of those attitudes one finds to be unproductive. Until a person knows what his attitudes are, he can neither accept nor modify them. Rogers (1951) pointed out that it is unlikely that a counselor can accept others unless he is also in the process of trying to accept himself. Elsewhere in that early volume (1951), Rogers and other authors pointed out that self-acceptance is a lifelong task which is never completed. They also pointed out that it is less important for counselors to be "finished products" as far as self-development is concerned than it is that they be willing to engage in the dual processes of understanding and accepting themselves while at the same time trying to make needed attitudinal changes.

As one explores one's attitudes, there are certain areas to consider. The first of these is how one views oneself and one's relationships with other persons, in this case, with parents.

I-THOU

Buber (1958) expressed his formulations about constructive and life giving attitudes toward self in relation to others when he discussed I–Thou relationships. Buber seems to have been a gentle philosopher who did not exhort others to do what he said they should do, but his ideas can be thoughtful challenges. Buber discussed contrasting attitudes: I–Thou and I–It. In the relationship in which one person (I) approaches another as Thou, the other person is valued as a being to be respected, and indeed, revered. In contrast, in the I–It relationship one approaches another as an object to be analyzed and dissected into parts or functions.

Buber pointed out that people live largely in a world of I–It, and certainly that kind of relationship is functional. For example, without some ability to analyze, one person would not know another person's eye or hair color, what the other person likes for dinner, and so forth. Buber also pointed out that a human being has the capacity for moments of I–Thou experience, when one person experiences another as a whole being which cannot be analyzed or dissected. He considered the I–Thou moments to prevent one person from violating another, and thus to prevent deterioration of relationships. While it is appropriate to have I–It moments, to dissect or analyze, the reverence one feels for those one can sometimes address as Thou precludes any attempt to manipulate or use them. Careful consideration of Buber's philosophy can lead a counselor to raise searching questions such as, "How often do I view parents as things to be dealt with?" and "Am I prone to see parents as objects to be manipulated for the benefit of their children?" or "How often do I revere the information I have to offer more than I revere the parent to whom I offer it?"

Buber's philosophy is similar to that expressed by Howe (1953). Howe believed that the order of the universe calls for man to love people and to use things, but that man often reverses the order and instead loves things and uses people. In Howe's view, this reversal creates problems, both for the person who uses others and for those being used.

AUTHORITY

In trying to live out relationships that acknowledge people as beings rather than as objects to be manipulated, it is also important to consider one's views about oneself as an authority. Each counselor must choose between viewing self as either what Fromm (1947, p. 9) termed a "rational authority" or an "irrational authority."

As Fromm explained it, the source of rational authority is competence. This authority is based upon the equality of both the authority and the "subject," that is, the person seeking help. The rational authority and the subject differ only in the degree of skill or knowledge each possesses in a particular area. Thus rational authority not only is earned, it must be conferred by others. For example, Miss Jones may have an area of expertise, say, physical therapy. But until others recognize her skills as a physical therapist they do not view her as an authority in the area, that is, they do not confer authority upon her.

Further, according to Fromm, the person using rational authority does not intimidate those who confer authority upon him; he does not demand their awe. Rather, rational authority asks for the constant scrutiny and criticism of those subjected to it.

Fromm also stated that rational authority is temporary. This makes sense when one understands that rational authority considers the knowledge of others, recognizes and welcomes new data, and sees others as having areas of expertise. Therefore that authority is likely from time to time to be overridden by the authority of others.

All readers probably have known persons who functioned as rational authorities. These persons were authorities by virtue of experience and knowledge but were also eager to learn from others, to admit their mistakes, to change their minds in the face of new information, and to try new ways of doing things. These people are usually remembered with respect and warmth because their ability to be unthreatened made them nonthreatening to others.

In contrast to rational authority, Fromm believed, irrational authority has its source in the desire for power over others. The power an irrational authority seeks can be either physical or mental, but the essential elements of this type of authority are the need for power over people and the necessity of inspiring their fear. Criticism is forbidden; when criticized, the irrational authority may become defensive and combative. Readers probably have known many of the people Fromm described as irrational authorities. These people seemed to assume they were always right, could not admit mistakes, could not tolerate criticism, and seemed to govern by fear. These people usually do not engender warm recollections.

Like Buber, Fromm seemed to postulate a dichotomy, an either –or attitude in which one is either one way or the other—in Fromm's case, either a rational or an irrational authority. It is obvious that no one lives at all times at either one end of the continuum or the other; no one is one hundred percent a rational authority or one hundred percent an irrational authority. Rather each person behaves more one way than the other at some times, and moves toward the other end of the continuum on other occasions. The important thing is to deal consciously with authority. When one understands the attitudes that are held, one can set out to keep or to change them.

I assume that parent counselors want to behave more often as rational authorities. They want to acknowledge the authority they have acquired by virtue of their experience, whatever this experience includes. Note here that one need not be an experienced counselor in order to have areas of authority. Those who are beginning counselors will draw on other expertise, such as the interpersonal skills developed through the process of living, while developing skills in counseling.

Counselors wishing to live out rational authority will be conscious of the equality between themselves and the parents with whom they work. They will not want parents to fear them. They will understand that parental questions and criticism are necessary if counselors are to continue to function as rational authorities.

Counselors using rational authority will also look upon parents as specialists. They will recognize clearly that, even as they are specialists in certain areas, each parent also has areas in which to exercise rational authority.

PARENTS AS SPECIALISTS

Specifically, each parent is a specialist in certain matters concerning his own child; each parent also is a specialist in his experience and perception of that child. The parent knows and interacts with a child at home and within a family. The parent's experience predates and exceeds the experience others have with the child. No other person will know a child in the ways his parents do.

Although counselors sometimes overlook such parental authority, the fact that parents are authorities seems obvious when you stop and think about it. For example, who knows more about the meaning of your birth to your mother than she does? Certainly neither her obstetrician nor her husband experienced your birth as she did. Who knows more about your father's view of his role in the family than your father? No one else could experience your father's life. Each person is an authority in his own right, and certainly parents of handicapped children know more than anyone else about their own experiences and their own perceptions of having and rearing that child.

It is suggested that counselors review their assumptions about their own authority and the authority of others. If one is tempted to view oneself as *the* authority and the parent as an untrained nonspecialist, or if one consistently views oneself as the authoritarian leader and the parent as a subject to be acted upon or used for one's own enhancement, these attitudes surely will be revealed in verbal or nonverbal behavior with parents. Furthermore, parents' perceptions of such attitudes will probably create such negative responses as defensiveness, resentment, or withdrawal. Counselors should consider their views about authority because they probably will fare better when they gratefully accept the fact that the roles of authority and subject are constantly changing; or to phrase it differently, counselors will get along better with parents when they understand that whenever one counselor meets with one parent, there are two specialists involved.

QUESTIONING COUNSELOR ATTITUDES

As one way of beginning to clearly identify their attitudes about themselves and others, counselors can try to answer a number of questions. Perhaps the first question should be, "Why do I want to see this particular parent?" This question can reveal a number of attitudes, such as the extent to which the counselor views the parent as Thou, and therefore a person worthy of immediate respect and concern, in contrast to viewing the parent as It, an object to be acted on because of a child's problem. Elsewhere I (1972) and others, such as Bice (1952), McDonald (1962), and Taylor (1976), have deplored the tendency of many counselors to be almost exclusively child-centered and have encouraged more attention to the needs of parents themselves. Parents can be viewed as clients, and counselors are encouraged to view them in this way.

Another question counselors might ask themselves is, "To what extent do I blame this parent for the child's problems?" This question will indicate the possible direction of counselor projection and bias.

This writer believes that a most important counselor question is, "To what extent do I believe I can solve this parent's problems?" Answers to this question will reveal the degree to which a counselor tends to exercise what the writer calls a "Jehovah complex." Many people seem to have at least a small desire to "play God." When this tendency or desire is present in a counselor, it will surface in verbal and nonverbal behavior, in choices between rational and irrational authority, in what the counselor asks parents to do, and in the counselor's feelings of success and satisfaction. The counselor who feels responsible for taking the lead in solving parents' problems is likely to give out great amounts of advice and to feel successful only with parents who act on such advice.

Counselors have an alternative to the attitude that they are responsible for managing the lives and problems of parents. Counselors can work to incorporate what Rogers (1951) first described as client-centered attitudes, that is, attitudes of respecting parents as individuals capable of managing their own lives, of clarifying those aspects that need changing, and of carrying out their own solutions. Purtile (1975) reminded counselors that there are ethical issues involved in choosing whether or not to assume responsibility for the life or the suffering of another.

SUMMARY

As counselors question their attitudes and assumptions about themselves, it will lead them to greater knowledge of their attitudes and assumptions about parents and about the very process of counseling. It seems important that counselors engage in such questioning. Because counseling is interpersonal communication, it is inevitable (a) that attitudes and assumptions will be conveyed in one's messages, and (b) that the meanings conveyed by attitudes and assumptions can override and obscure any message content. Counselors who understand these facts will carefully prepare the content of counseling sessions, but first and foremost they will carefully attend to the attitudes they bring to any session.

Again it is stressed that one's attitudes need not be completely "fixed-up" in order to engage in parent counseling. Instead, the counselor's goals should include increased understanding and acceptance of self, coupled with willingness to change, grow, and develop. Such openness, self-acceptance, and willingness to change are requisites for counselors who wish to be accepting of parents.

STUDY GUIDES FOR CHAPTER 3

Additional Readings

Buber, M. *I and thou* (2nd ed.), (R. Smith., trans.). New York: Charles Scribner's Sons, 1958. Part I.

Fromm, E. *Escape from freedom.* New York: Holt, 1947, pp. 8–14.

Johnson, D. *Reaching out: Interpersonal effectiveness and self-actualization.* Englewood Cliffs, New Jersey: Prentice Hall, 1972, chap. 8.

Purtile, R. *Essays for professional helpers.* Thorofare, New Jersey: Charles B. Slack, 1975, pp. 49–52.

Rogers, C. *Client-centered therapy* (paperback ed.). Boston: Houghton-Mifflin, 1965, chap. 2.
Taylor, F. Project cope. In E. Webster (Ed.), *Professional approaches with parents of handicapped children*. Springfield: Charles C. Thomas, 1976, pp. 146–152.

Practice Exercises

1. As a way of becoming more aware of your areas of authority and of areas in which parents are authorities:
    A. Think about a child you have known quite well, perhaps a child you have worked with or are now working with. List information you have about the child that his parents may not know or may not understand. Make a second list of information the parents have about the child that you have no way of knowing except by asking the parent. You may wish to include in the first list experiences you have had that the parent has not had. Likewise, in the second list, you may wish to include experiences the parent has had with the child that you have not had.
    B. Imagine that you wish to behave as a rational authority while with a parent. List 10 to 12 statements or questions you might use to reveal your attitudes of respect for your authority and for the parent's. Be sure to read each utterance aloud, because your attitudes are revealed as much by how you say things as by what you say. Modify each utterance until you feel satisfied that it is a fairly brief and accurate expression of rational authority.
    C. The statement was made in the text that you need not be an experienced counselor to have areas in which you are an authority. List six to eight areas in which you are an authority by virtue of your own unique experience.
2. The writer listed several questions counselors might ask themselves as they attempt to become more aware of their attitudes. From your experience, list several other questions by which one might explore one's attitudes.

PART II

Improving Counselor Communication

There are many additional variables that enter into counselor–parent communication. Several are discussed in this section. Attention to these matters can result in more effective counselor communication and thus lead to more effective parent counseling.

4

Listening

As the term is used here, listening to another person encompasses a great deal more activity than just hearing what the person says. Listening involves the extremely complicated processes of perceiving, attending to, and noting another's nonverbal and verbal behaviors.

One listens to another person with one's own inner world in action to create perceptual sets and attitudes toward the other person. These attitudes influence not only the amount and kind of material received, they also determine one's responses to that material. For example, one can listen to the conversation of another while feeling critical of him and no doubt find items judged worthy of criticism. In this case one probably will make verbal or nonverbal responses that reflect one's attitudes of criticism; one may argue, disagree, or in some way try to refute what the other person says. On the other hand, when one listens to another while set to approve or agree, one is likely to note those items of which one approves and to respond with some type of agreement; such agreement can be veiled or it can be openly stated.

One's attitudes are subject to sudden change, and it is very common to listen while feeling critical one moment and feeling approval a moment later. It should be noted, however, that when either an attitude of criticism or one of approval is at the forefront, one's verbal or nonverbal responses will be evaluative. That is, in the case of either agreement or disagreement, one has made a judgment that will be expressed in some form of evaluative behavior.

LISTENING TO UNDERSTAND

It also is possible to listen to another while holding what this writer calls an inquiring attitude. This is an attitude of wishing to find out about the other person, to know and understand as fully as possible what the world of the other is like. Such an attitude results in the behavior of listening to try to understand. Listening to understand involves delaying judgment long enough to catch a glimpse of what the other person thinks or feels. When one listens in this way, one is not set to agree or disagree. Rather, one is set to attend to and try to glimpse more fully the ideas, attitudes, and emotions expressed by the other. Listening to understand, then, involves trying *not to:* one tries *not to* judge until well after one has listened nonjudgmentally to the other. When one listens nonjudgmentally, one will not use evaluative responses and thus will learn more about the other person. Rogers (1951; 1965) called such inquiring attitudes *client-centered,* and Gordon (1970) referred to the behaviors associated with listening to understand as *active listening.* Numerous examples of such behaviors were given by Benjamin (1974) in his book on interviewing.

It is understood that listening to understand is a difficult task, but it can be learned. Furthermore, if counselors wish to establish and maintain productive and satisfying relationships with parents, it is essential that they learn to listen in this way. Part of the task of developing greater skill as a listener is to become increasingly aware of one's own inner states and outer behaviors, and no doubt each reader has engaged in listening inquiringly. So it is not a new behavior to be learned, but a behavior that can be used with greater frequency.

In developing the ability to listen understandingly, counselors should first remember that no one can hold an inquiring attitude one hundred percent of the time; no one can hold any attitude all of the time. Rather, counselors should seek to hold an inquiring attitude more often.

It is also impossible to attain the goal expressed by many counselors as "forgetting myself and concentrating only on the other person." It is possible to listen almost exclusively to one's own inner promptings, and probably all readers have had the experience of being so lost in thought as to be unaware of what was happening in the outer world. However, when one considers how the very presence of another person activates one's own noise-making internal stimuli, it is clear that it is impossible to rule oneself out of the interaction and to listen *only* to another person. Rather than trying to rule the self out, it is more realistic to seek the goal of using internal stimuli to assist listening. Counselors can use their constantly active internal stimuli to attend to more of what parents say, to notice more behavioral cues that parents give them, and to use these cues to formulate hypotheses.

Formulating and Testing Hypotheses

The formulation of hypotheses—that is, guesses or hunches—requires the listener from time to time to try to put into his own words what he thinks the other person is saying. The counselor should not try to repeat or parrot the parent's words. As Garrett (1942) pointed out, the most effective responses will probably be original constructions, expressing the counselor's wish to glimpse not only the content but also possible meanings of the other person's verbal and nonverbal communication.

In formulating and testing hypotheses, counselors should be aware of not only the vast individual differences between people but also the commonalities shared by all human beings. Such similarities are not to be found in the area of shared experiences where there is little commonality. No two people share all the same experiences; even when two people are in the same situation, they experience it differently. The common bonds between people are to be found in the area of emotions. All people have at one time or another experienced all the emotions known to human beings; all people have experienced hurt, anger, loneliness, satisfaction, pleasure, pride, and so forth. Because a counselor and a parent are bound to have experienced similar emotions, the counselor can use his own world to formulate hypotheses about the possible contents of a parent's world.

Hypotheses are tentative; they are expressions of one's

hunches or guesses and should be treated as such. Furthermore, the accuracy of a hypothesis should be tested. Gordon (1970) used the term *active listening* to include listening inquiringly and stating hypotheses.

The following example illustrates such active listening. Mrs. B's words should be read rather tentatively; they are, after all, only her guesses and should not be read as dogmatic pronouncements. The parents' discussion centered first on the ending of a 10-week speech therapy session for their children, and then on their experience in six parent group meetings; this series also was ending.

MRS. A: I sure hate to see this session end.

MRS. B: Now you'll have the twins under foot all the time.

MRS. A: [laughing] Sure will. It has been so good for them to be separated, and so peaceful! But I'll miss seeing you people too [referring to other persons in the group].

MRS. B: This is about the best adult conversation we have in a day, isn't it?

MRS. A: Yeah, you people really have been good for me, and it's good to talk adult-talk, about things that matter to adults. I've enjoyed it.

Mrs. B made guesses about the meanings of Mrs. A's words and expressed thoughts about content that Mrs. A had not yet stated. Mrs. B's manner indicated that she knew these were only guesses. The writer believes counselors will find it useful to be aware of times when they behave as Mrs. B did and to practice verbalizing their guesses more often.

When one makes hunches about the world of another person, it is relatively unimportant whether the guess is right or wrong. Mrs. B happened to be right, and that is fine. On another occasion Mrs. B might be wrong, and that's fine too. The important thing in trying to formulate and test hypotheses is to persevere in doing so. Over and over again, parents report that they cannot remember exactly what such a listener said, but they can remember feeling that the listener was "really listening and understanding."

When counselors listen nonjudgmentally, they have little need to question whether or not certain topics are appropriate for parental discussion. They assume that anything of importance in a parent's world is appropriate to discuss, if the parent wishes to so do. The counselor who listens to understand recognizes that a parent can make the judgment regarding the appropriateness and relevance of a topic. Mrs. D's conversation in the following example illustrates this point. She and a counselor had been talking about her difficulties as she tried to communicate with her son Jerry, a boy of 10, who talked with her very little. The conversation took place during a sustained period of extremely hot and humid weather.

MRS. D: Of course if this weather doesn't change, I don't know what's going to become of us.

C: You react badly to heat?

MRS. D: Oh gosh, I just can't take it. I get so depressed because I just feel bad. I can't *move.* And our air conditioning at home isn't enough to cool the house. . . . I've asked the landlord to put in a larger central unit. . . . I'd move if I could find another place that would be close to the boys' school . . . or maybe I wouldn't have the energy to move.

C: Moving would take more energy than you have right now.

MRS. D: Yes. The whole situation makes me so anxious. The doctor has given me Valium, but I'm scared to take it four times a day like he says I should. . . . I'm not much for pills to solve my problems.

C: Sort of like they only delay the time when you have to face the issues.

MRS. D: Well, yes, and sometimes they [pills] change the issues. Look at the kids these days. . . . You know, it sounds like we're talking about trivia here—the weather, moving, pills—but it all relates.

C: This is a big part of your life right now, isn't it?

MRS. D: It seems like my whole life. And I know I'm worse with Jerry when I feel so awful.

Counselors who grant parents the right to discuss topics of importance to them are not simply laissez faire leaders. Such counselors are extremely active in following the parent's thoughts and feelings.

As counselors listen, they may wonder why a parent has raised a given topic for discussion and question its relevance to the parent. Such counselor wondering can be verbalized. There are numerous ways to inquire about meanings, two examples of which follow.

MRS. W: Let me tell you about Clara B . . . She . . .

C: I guess I don't understand what's important to you about Clara B.

MRS.W: Not much, really. It's just a smoke screen to keep from talking about what's really bugging me.

MRS. L: My sister called last night, the one who has been sick for so long. She was all upset, crying.

C: What did the call do to you?

MRS. L: I felt so helpless. What could I say to her now? I guess it really broke my heart that she wasn't getting any better, and I had prayed so much that she would be.

C: *Awful* powerless feeling, wasn't it?

MRS. L: [tears in eyes] Oh, just awful, I must have cried for an hour afterwards.

C: [getting Kleenex] What a tragedy! Does it help to talk about it?

MRS. L: Well, it's awful to feel torn up, and the kids don't understand. . . . I just hurt!

Note that in the examples the counselor did not state, nor seem to imply, "That's not important; we're here to talk about your child." The counselor respected those topics the parent thought important.

Counselors sometimes fear that when given opportunities to discuss topics of their choice, parents will fail to discuss their handicapped children. Quite the contrary is true. Because these children are such major factors in their parents' lives, parental conversation will probably center on them for much of the counseling time.

Although it may sound paradoxical, part of the listening counselor's task is to introduce topics. When counselors are sensitive to parental worlds, they hear questions that need to be answered and ideas that need to be elaborated. When counselors think a topic should be pursued, it is better to raise it in direct fashion—to send a congruent message—than to wait for the time when parents themselves might happen to raise it. Counselors who suggest a topic for discussion also should listen to and acknowledge verbal and nonverbal parental responses that indicate whether or not they want to discuss the item. Some topics can be threatening, at least momentarily; other topics simply are not important to parents at a certain time. When people do not want to discuss a subject, they give off various signals to indicate their feelings. The listening counselor learns to pay attention to these cues.

Silence

A discussion of listening to understand would not be complete if no mention were made of silence. Silence is very often threatening to counselors, usually because they see it as a sign of resistance. Benjamin (1974) spoke of several reasons for silence, only one of which was resistance. Another factor prompting silence is the need to think about information, to absorb it. People also need time to formulate questions or statements, and often this activity can best be done in silence. Finally, silence can offer a means of coping with a rush of emotions, giving a person a chance to return to a state of greater composure.

In light of the above factors, silence can be seen to be very beneficial. Rather than being so uncomfortable with silence as to try to avoid it at all costs, counselors can practice sitting quietly in periods of silence. Silence can be useful to counselors as well as to parents, first because counselors need to engage in the types of mental activity described above, and also because counselors can use silent periods for the type of hunch-making discussed above.

WHAT COUNSELORS HEAR WHEN THEY LISTEN TO PARENTS

As counselors listen to parents, they catch glimpses of the rich texture of human frailty and indomitable strength. Counselors learn that, taken as a group, parents of handicapped children are not seriously emotionally disturbed people. Like all other human beings, they struggle with existential anxieties and problems. They also experience joy, satisfaction, and success. They seek to live satisfying and productive lives as individuals. As Heisler (1972) stated, they confront all of the internal events—anxiety, shock, disappointment, fear, joy, and hope—that are part of living. In addition, the fact of being a parent creates additional pressures to compound the problems faced by any human being.

Parents of handicapped children have revealed themselves to be similar to other parents in many respects. They want to do what they think is right for their children. They would like to see themselves as good parents, and they would like others to view them in this light. Parents of handicapped children are also unique in many ways; they face certain crises and continuing pressures unknown to parents of children who are not disabled.

Experience of Crisis

Counselors should be aware that the discovery of a disorder in their child can consitute a crisis for many parents, even when the disorder is judged to be mild. Furthermore, parents may go through several stages of reaction to crisis before arriving at a point of being able to participate actively in their children's training or education. The four stages of reaction to crisis postulated by Shontz (1965) can be related to the parents of a handicapped child in the following way.

Shock.   On learning of a child's problem, the parent experiences shock. This period can be brief or it can last for a longer time. Shock can bring numbness, a sense of unreality, and disbelief.

Realization.   Shock is followed by realization, or an awareness of the reality of the situation. Realization can be accompanied by acute anxiety which still prevents a parent from perceiving accurately. Parents may seem fearful, easily upset or annoyed, or give some such indication that their anxiety level is very high.

Defensive Retreat.   In the stage of defensive retreat, the parent attempts to avoid coping with the anxiety-producing situation. Anxiety is such a painful emotion that people defend against it in whatever ways they can; retreat is one means of defense. In the period of retreat, the parent may look to others—an institution, a professional person, a clinic—to take over responsibility for the child. It is as if the parent is saying, "I can't cope with this situation."

Acknowledgment.   Retreat can be followed by the stage of acknowledgment. With acknowledgment, and in spite of anxiety and disappointment, the parent can mobilize inner forces to cope with the situation. The parent can now become an active participant in the various services provided for the child.

Lowell (1965) and Simmons-Martin (1976) applied these ideas about reaction to crisis to parents of hearing-impaired children. It seems quite likely that parents of children with other handicaps follow a similar pattern (Group for the Advancement of Psychiatry, 1973), so that these stages apply to them as well. For example, parental shock with its dulling of perception may account in part for the common counselor experience of having to repeat information because it was not understood when first presented. Parents who seem disinterested, break appointments, or do not carry out home training activities may be in the period of defensive retreat, with acknowledgment still extremely painful.

Note that the definition of acknowledgment does not include the word *acceptance*. There are many aspects of life that a person cannot accept but can learn to adjust to and cope with. In light of a parent's hopes and dreams for a perfect child, Simmons-Martin (1976) recognized that the parent can feel deep grief when the child is found to be defective, and may need to experience a period of mourning. Other authors, including Bice (1952), Wing (1972), Raymond, Slaby, and Lieb (1975), and Buscaglia (1975) considered it unrealistic to expect a parent to accept the child's handicap, if to accept means to feel agreeable about. Rather, a parent can be helped to acknowledge the imperfect area and to cope with it, while also recognizing and affirming the more perfect dimensions of the child.

Concerns

Parents of children with handicaps share a universe of concerns with those whose children are developing normally. All parents seem concerned about their children's social development, educational future, and ability to function with increasing independence. Parents of handicapped children express these same concerns.

I have reported previously (1974) on the concerns expressed by a sample of parents of children with communication handicaps. Their most frequently voiced worries were about their children's future socialization and education. In fact, these parents seemed to want counselors to provide information about the children's disorders in the context of explanations of how these details related to long-term socialization and education. In later studies (1976) of a larger sample, including both mothers and fathers of children with various types of disorders, the pattern of parental concerns remained the same: Parents were primarily concerned about their children's social development and potential for education. Hunter and Shucman (1967) and Shelton (1972) reported the same concerns in parents of retarded children, and Bice (1952) was one of the early counselors who recognized these concerns in mothers of children with cerebral palsy.

While sharing concerns common to all parents, those whose children are handicapped also have different concerns, just by virtue of having to provide for a child who is different. It is a hurtful thing to have a handicapped child; it is also confusing. Perhaps, as Heisler (1972) suggested, the very presence of a handicapped child in the family intensifies any problems that parents would experience. Or perhaps, as Satir (1967) suggested, parents of children with disorders find that their children serve as a focal point for their problems. In any case, parents of children with handicaps have different strains imposed by having to provide for their children's special treatment or education. For example, many parents have children with dental problems, but parents of children with cleft palates may have particular difficulty in locating dentists and providing for regular and usually extensive dental help. As another example all parents want their children to develop motor skills, but the parent of a child with cerebral palsy usually must seek special treatment to help the child develop motorically. As a final example, the desire of all parents for their children's education can lead to a series of disappointments and frustrations for parents of children with learning disabilities.

Many parents voice concern about the possibility of overprotecting their children. They fear they will go beyond the fine line of providing needed protection and slip into the state of constantly trying to protect. Counselors often hear such statements as, "I don't want to spoil him," or "I know we can't protect him from all of life's hurts, but I'm afraid I try to." A father expressed it as, "It's hard not to overprotect. I'd like to protect my little girl from any more problems. She already has her share."

A concern expressed by many parents, particularly mothers, is how to provide adequately for the needs of the handicapped child and those of other family members (Barsch, 1968; 1970a; 1970b; Shelton, 1972; Taylor, 1976; Doernberg, Bernard, and Lenz, 1976). Perhaps this concern is more widespread among mothers of the severely disabled, but the writer has heard it discussed as well by women of children with mild disorders. There is a need for family harmony and equilibrium. The need to focus attention on one family member easily disrupts such equilibrium, often creating friction and inharmonious relationships. Such unilateral parental involvement with one child can contribute to marital problems, and many authors such as Satir (1967), McDonald (1962), Heisler (1972), Doernberg, Bernard, and Lenz (1967), and Taylor (1976) have noted the potential for marital discord in families where children present problems.

Fathers as well as mothers express concern when perceiving either their own or their spouse's overinvolvement. The following parental statements are illustrative.

MRS. P: I wish I could find a happy medium. My older boys think I love Sam better than them because I spend so much time taking him to the speech clinic and helping him with his speech. My husband gives me a hard time sometimes too, when I tell him to pay attention to Sam. Last night I told him to listen to Sam and he said, "Why? Nobody pays attention to me." I'm in the middle, and I don't know where it leads.

MR. B: She [his wife] has so much time and emotional energy invested in George [the son with a severe reading problem] that it's a drain on her. I worry about what it's going to do to all of us in the family.

MR. C: We've both [he and his wife] been so tied up with trying to do right by Ernie [a child with Down's syndrome] that we're only beginning to realize that we've been overlooking what the other kids need. We're beginning to realize they have been feeling left out.

Aspirations

When counselors listen, they also hear about parents' aspirations for themselves and for their children. I believe that parents want to be good parents, and generally they want to be better than they are. It seems that human beings desire to grow and develop, and parents express this aspiration in numerous ways.

Just as parents express the wish for their own improvement, they want and need to talk about their hopes for their children's lives. Murphy (1976) wrote with great sensitivity about ways in which counselors can help parents of handicapped children to sustain hope while still being realistic about the prognoses for their

children. Hope is essential to human life. But in order to be nourish-
ing, hope must be tempered with awareness and understanding.
Listening counselors can help parents arrive at such greater awareness and understanding. More will be said about this in Chapter 10,
which discusses the issue of clarification.

Guilt

Guilt is closely related to parental aspirations for themselves. It
is a very human characteristic to set one's goals so high that one
cannot reach them. Often parents hold unattainable goals and guilt
follows repeated failure to live up to their own standards. Also, other
persons are prone to give these parents advice, much of which may
be very good. In addition to well-meaning family members, neigh-
bors, and other unprofessional advisors, parents are subject to
quantities of advice on child rearing through reading newspaper or
magazine articles. Conscientious parents will often try to follow
suggestions made by those whose lives are vastly different from
their own or who differ from each other in the theoretical position
from which they speak. The more diligently parents try to follow
such conflicting suggestions, the more likely it is that they will be
confused, will fail, and will feel some degree of guilt.

Guilt feelings are experienced by all people, and whether parents of handicapped children experience more guilt than other persons is not known. However it is known that guilt is prevalent among
these parents. Many of them blame themselves for their children's
problems; they seem convinced that they caused the disorder or
at least contributed to it. This is particularly true in cases where no
organic problem can be found to account for the disorder, but such
feelings are also expressed by parents of children with known organic deficits (McDonald, 1962; Doernberg et al, 1976). It is as if
these parents were saying, "I have got to think of a reason for
this, and in the absence of a clear reason, it must be my fault."
For example, during a parents' discussion, the mother of an adopted
child with a learning disability said, "Sometimes I feel so guilty that
I have caused Harry's problems; then I stop and think how crazy
that is. I didn't even know Harry until he was 2 years old, and if it's
true that these problems start before that, I couldn't be to blame
because I didn't have anything to do with him so early." Several

other members agreed that her guilt was unrealistic, but one said, "I know how it is, sometimes you just look around trying to find *something* you think you did wrong."

Guilt can be stirred by the perception that any behavior is not up to one's standards, or that such behavior will have negative consequences. Thus parents may feel guilty when they show anger toward their children, or when they even feel angry, or when they feel discouraged about them and wish to be away from them for a time. The feeling that they are not providing adequately for other family members stirs guilt. Parents who must perform special tasks in their children's treatment or education may feel guilty when they grow weary of doing them or feel they are extremely difficult to do.

Parental guilt can be expressed in an infinite number of ways. Parents may say directly, "I feel guilty about . . ." but more often they express such feelings more indirectly. For example, a father said, "I often wonder what we did to deserve this," and a mother told a counselor, "It seems I am being punished by having a child with cerebral palsy." Such parental verbalizations suggest a number of emotions, one of which may be guilt. Such statements as, "I have tried so hard, but I just can't . . ." or "I think I could, but I just can't . . ." can signal that a parent may be feeling guilt.

Joy and Success

Although parents of handicapped children experience numerous stresses and strains, it is erroneous to think that their lives contain only negative experiences or emotions. Of course this is not true. These parents experience success. They feel joy, hope, satisfaction, and happiness. Many exhibit a highly developed sense of humor and their laughter is frequent and genuine.

Curious as it may seem to some counselors, the child with the handicap can be a source of good feelings as well as a source of hurt and concern. Many parents report feelings of success and great satisfaction when they help their children make progress. For example, one mother said, "When you have worked so hard to help make changes, any progress is a cause for celebration." Parents express deep love for their children. As one mother put it, "My love is more and bigger than all the hurt and hair pulling."

When counselors listen, they can hear parents express their

good feelings in a variety of unique ways; they can recognize parental humor, and note expressions of joy, satisfaction, and good feelings. These positive feelings are as much the stuff of life as are
worries and concerns. Counselors who listen actively to the contents of parents' worlds cannot become so problem-oriented that
they overlook or ignore the positive aspects of parents' lives.

SUMMARY

Among the important things counselors can do to improve their
communication with parents is to offer themselves as listeners. Listening has the additional benefit of further educating counselors.
There are various attitudes with which one listens to another person,
and special attention was given in this chapter to developing the
ability to listen to understand. Counselors who listen with attitudes
of trying to understand engage in the process of formulating and
testing hypotheses. These hypotheses are tested by verbalizing
them.

When counselors listen to parents of handicapped children,
they hear about the experience of crisis, parental concerns, levels of
aspiration, and guilt. They also hear parents express feelings of joy,
happiness, success, and satisfaction.

STUDY GUIDES FOR CHAPTER 4

Additional Readings

Benjamin, A. *The helping interview* (2nd ed.). Boston: Houghton Mifflin,
    1974, Chapter 3.
Gordon, T. *Parent effectiveness training.* New York: Peter H. Wyden, 1970,
    Chapter 3.
Johnson, D. *Reaching out: Interpersonal effectiveness and self actualiza-
    tion.* Englewood Cliffs, New Jersey: Prentice-Hall, 1972, Chapter 7.

Practice Exercises

1. Listen to a brief conversation between two people; you may be a participant in the conversation or you may be an eavesdropper. In either case your task is to listen to try to understand meanings expressed by another person. You will try to formulate hypotheses about what another person thinks or feels, but in this exercise you do not need to try to test your hypotheses by verbalizing them. The first important step in listening to understand is to be aware of and identify your hunches.

2. As a second step in the practice of listening to understand, engage in a brief conversation with one other person. This time try to make hunches about what the other person may be thinking and feeling *and also* try to verbalize your hunches.

3. List at least six ways that a person might send the message, "I don't want to discuss this topic any further."

5

Establishing the Counselor–Parent
Contract

THE IMPORTANCE OF STRUCTURE AND LIMITS

People often think of structure or limits as negative necessities of life. Many persons have professed to have an aversion to any limits. Rather than being aversive, structure and limits are highly desirable if a person is to function well. Each person needs a sense of order and structure in his life. This is not to say that all people are well organized or orderly, or even that the best organized and most orderly person is that way at all times. Rather, people need the security of knowing that there is some structure around which they can organize their lives. People seldom think about it, perhaps, but they would feel extremely insecure if they could not be relatively sure that the sun would rise and set with regularity, or if they never knew when mealtime might be or when they might see their friends. While everyone enjoys participating in spontaneous events from time to time, it would be anxiety producing if everything in their lives were unplanned, unstructured, and unlimited.

Fromm (1947) made the point that human beings can experience freedom only as they know the limits by which such freedom is bounded. One's need for the freedom provided by knowledge of limits seems obvious when one stops to think about it. For example, when you are going to a movie or a class, you want to know when it starts, because only then are you free to choose whether to be on time or to arrive late. Or you may be one who likes to have people call before they drop in to visit so that you are free to prepare or not to prepare for the visit. There are numerous other examples of the freedom provided by limits: highway speed limits give one a choice of adhering to them or testing them; house plant fanciers want to have directions for the amount of light and water to give them so that they can be free to enjoy their plants rather than worrying about them; and one checks weather reports to assess the type of clothing that will provide freedom from cold, heat, or wetness.

Conversely, everyone has probably experienced the uncertain, annoyed, perhaps powerless feelings accompanying too little structure, that is, too few limits. Perhaps you have arrived for a meeting only to find it had been re-scheduled, or you may have participated in a meeting that was scheduled to end at a certain hour and experienced the feelings of frustration and annoyance as the meeting went on for an additional hour. You may be one who reacts negatively to the person who often says, "Come see me!" but always neglects to say when. In situations like these, people become at least uncomfortable; they may also become very anxious and annoyed.

Note that in many of the above examples, the element of time is important. Benjamin (1974) made the point that people structure a great deal of their lives in terms of time. He stated further that having a sense of time limits can lead one to feel secure, and thereby can help one to be himself. Benjamin's ideas were similar to Fromm's notion that one can feel freedom only within limits. Following the ideas of these authors, when one knows the limitations of a situation (particularly time limits), it is as if one could say, "I am free to be myself for this period of time."

Matters of structure and limits are important considerations for parent counselors as they plan for their interaction with parents. And counselors have the initial responsibility for planning because parents simply have no basis for knowing what to expect, and therefore what to plan.

In a real sense counselors contract, or enter into agreements with parents about what the structure of their time together will be. Counselors know their intentions in meeting with any parent and they can plan and contract for limits to be placed both on themselves and on parents. A counselor's verbalization of an appropriate number of specific statements about structure and limits is necessary to establish the contract with a given parent.

STATING THE CONTRACT

The counselor's share of the contract is stated early in the first session. If the counselor and parent are to see each other for just one session, the contract is binding for one session only. If they will meet for a series of sessions, the initial contract can cover the entire series. Counselors state some form of contract no matter who has requested the conference; that is, whether the counselor has asked to see a parent or the parent has asked for the meeting. In either case it is necessary to establish a structure for the meeting. However the variable of who requested the meeting influences at least one of the basic elements of the contract; this matter will be discussed in a later section.

The counselor's task in stating the contract is to outline those details that a parent needs to know, and to say only that much. A counselor's temptation can be to spell out every detail, thereby inundating the parent with information. A counselor can suspect that he is oververbalizing when he hears himself engaging in a mono-logue. Any time that counselors talk too much during parent inter-views, it can create an uncomfortable situation for all participants. Therefore counselors should guard against talking too much or for a longer time than is necessary.

As a safeguard against counselor monologue, counselors are encouraged to practice ways of stating the contract simply and briefly, then to open the discussion to other matters that are impor-tant to consider at the initial meeting. Another safeguard is to en-courage parental discussion of contractual elements as they are being presented.

Spontaneity is another factor to be considered in the way the counselor states the contract. Beginning counselors have often tried to write down all their contractual statements as a safeguard against omitting anything of importance; this preparation is worthwhile. However, when counselors have read their prepared statements or have stated the contract as it was committed to memory, most often they have been dissatisfied with their performance. One such counselor stated, "I sounded like a computer, not a person." Although it seems imperative that one make notes about the facts to be stated, one can practice using a conversational manner to deliver these messages.

BASIC ELEMENTS OF THE CONTRACT

Perhaps the basic elements of any counselor–parent contract can best be summarized as answers to the following questions: (a) "How much time do we have at this visit or at future visits?" (b) "Why are we here?" (c) "Who will be involved in this visit or future visits?" and (d) "What will we be doing?" It may be necessary in individual situations to mention other factors, but these four seem to be the essentials. The counselor will not necessarily answer the questions in the order in which they are presented here, and he can combine answers into sentences that give the parent more than one item of information. However each question will be discussed separately here, then answers will be combined into sample contractual statements.

How Much Time Do We Have?

The counselor can speak generally of time or can refer to a specific starting and ending time. Examples follow.

1. "We have the time from now until 3 o'clock." (specific)
2. "We have the next half-hour to talk."   (specific)
3. "We will use this hour every week."   (specific)
4. "We can schedule an hour each week."   (general)
5. "We can schedule half-hour appointments on one Friday of each month."   (general)
6. "We will meet for this half-hour on the first Friday of each month."   (specific)

Note in the above examples that when the counselor speaks generally about time, it seems to suggest possibilities. In examples 4 and 5, the counselor seems to suggest, "I have this time to see you if you like." Once the counselor has made a specific appointment or series of appointments with a parent, the counselor should indicate a definite commitment by speaking specifically about time.

In stating time limits, the counselor can also state simply whether this is planned as a one-time interview or as the first of several. Notice that in examples 1 and 2 the counselor makes no mention of future meetings, implying that this is a one-time interview. In the remaining examples the possibility of future meetings is either stated or implied; it seems clear that future meetings are, or can be, planned. Counselors who intend to have a series of meetings should say how many are planned; for example, "We will meet from 10 o'clock to 10:50 each Wednesday morning for 8 weeks."

Why Are We Here?

The purpose of a meeting or series of meetings with a parent can be stated very simply, but here the matter of who requested the session must be considered. As Benjamin (1974) pointed out, parents who request an interview will know what they want to discuss and the counselor will not know. Conversely, when counselors ask for the conference, only they will know the reason. In the former case the counselor might make a statement like, "I'm interested in hearing what you'd like to discuss with me." In the latter case there are also many options. For example, "I have asked you to come here so that we could discuss results of the testing done on your child," or "I asked you to meet with me so that we could discuss any changes you might have noticed in George's school performance," or "I have planned a weekly meeting during which we can exchange information and discuss various issues."

Counselors will experience fewer problems in a given interview if they remember who asked for the interview, and therefore, who already knows the purpose of the meeting. Problems can arise for the counselor who asks to see a parent, then behaves as if the parent knows the reason for the conference. Both parent and counselor would be very uncomfortable if the conversation followed a path like the one in the example below.

C: You know I asked you to come in to discuss the problems John is having in school.

P: No, I didn't know that.
C: You didn't know John is having problems?
P: Oh yes, John has always had trouble with his reading. I didn't know you wanted to talk with me about John's reading.
C: Well, I do.
P: Oh.

Here the counselor knew the reason for the interview but spoke as if the parent also knew it. Misunderstanding could have been avoided if the counselor had stated the purpose directly: "I asked you to come in so that we could discuss the problems John is having with reading." The parent might not have liked the topic, but at least would have had a chance to hear the topic immediately.

On the other hand, the counselor will experience problems if, in spite of being unaware of the reason that a parent asked for a conference, he behaves as if knowledgeable about the topic. For example, the counselor can feel foolish when he says confidently, "I'm sure you wanted to see me about John's school problems," and the parent says, "No, I didn't."

Counselors can avoid such scenes by remembering that only they know their reasons for requesting a meeting with parents and that they should quickly reveal these reasons. Conversely, when parents ask for conferences, only the parents know definitely what the topic is. In the latter case the counselor can say something like, "I'm interested in what you want to see me about," and thereby reveal both interest and ability to delay judgment.

Who Is Or Will Be Involved in the Counseling Sessions?

When the counseling situation is to involve only one counselor and one or several parents, an explanation of who will participate in the meetings is superfluous; "We will meet together," covers the subject. When persons other than the counselor and the parent(s) are to be participants, either regularly or from time to time, their presence should be explained. Ideally, the explanation of such visitors should be a part of the initial contract. Often, however, it is impossible to predict who may visit a session. In such cases the presence of visitors should be explained as soon as possible. Following are examples of three cases in which there are additional participants expected to attend counseling sessions, with two possible counselor explanations in each case.

In a large city school, parents of children with language, speech, and hearing problems and a counselor who was trained in speech pathology met for 2 hours on the first Friday afternoon of each month. Every other month the program included a consultant—a psychologist, social worker, physician, or special education supervisor.

1. Possible counselor explanation: "We will meet regularly from 1 to 3 o'clock on the first Friday of each month. At every other meeting we will have one additional person meet with us—either a psychologist, a social worker, a doctor, or a special teacher."

2. Possible counselor explanation: "In addition to those of us who are regulars in this group, every other month we will be joined by one consultant. We have scheduled a visit by a psychologist, a social worker, a pediatrician, and a special education specialist."

In a university training center, graduate students participated in each of eight weekly 1-hour parent group meetings.

1. Possible counselor explanation: "These people [introducing them] are students who want to learn about helping parents as well as helping children. They will meet with us regularly to share their ideas with you as well as learn from you about what they might do to assist you and other parents they will work with later."

2. Possible counselor explanation: "These students [introducing them] are assistants in this group. They will be participants in each session, and want to share their ideas with you as well as to learn how you think they can help families of handicapped children."

The superintendent of a large city school system was interested in visiting all school programs and meeting the people involved in them. He was planning to visit one of the monthly Wednesday evening parent meetings.

1. Possible counselor explanation: "I expect that sometime during one of our meetings we will have a visit from Mr. Meeks, the superintendent of schools. He sometimes drops in

to meet people and to ask their ideas for improving school programs. He does not plan to stay very long, but will be interested in what you have to say about your children's programs. We will interrupt our discussion so he can talk with you and continue it after he leaves."

2. Possible counselor explanation: "Mr. Meeks, the superintendent, whom some of you know, sometimes drops in to visit these groups to meet people who are here and to have a few minutes to visit. Should he drop in, we'll table our conversation so that you can talk with him, then continue it after he leaves."

The counselor should try to hold down the number of drop-in visitors. Drop-ins usually interrupt the work that is going on in a session. It seems obvious that only those who are regular participants in the sessions are entitled to share whatever privileged information may be forthcoming, and it is for this reason that both of the counselor's explanations in the above examples include the decision to interrupt the regular work of the group until the visitor leaves. Although a counselor cannot control all interruptions, he can exert considerable control over what happens while the interrupter is present.

What Will We Do?

Here the counselor explains whatever factors constitute integral parts of the session(s). Although most counselor–parent interactions follow a discussion format, there may be adjunctive activities or other variables that will take place. If so, the parent needs to know about them.

For example, many parent programs include research or training components, and the parent should know at the beginning when these are part of their program. If the parents are to fill out a pre- and postcounseling questionnaire or take a pre- and posttest, the counselor should explain why they are being asked to do so. Explanation also should be given about the use(s) of the information learned.

When a session is to be recorded on audiotape, videotape, or by an observer, a full explanation should be given. The writer believes it is unethical to record conversations when people are unaware that they are being recorded, but that recording of interviews can be very desirable because counselors can learn a great deal from studying tapes of their sessions. However it is imperative that each counselor decide whether or not to record a given counseling session rather than thinking of recording as a standard procedure which takes no prior thought. Although recording can be very useful in research or training, it usually is not helpful per se to the immediate counselor–parent interaction. Further, counselors should remember that many parents fear disclosing themselves to others, and a tape recorder may increase their reticence. Counselors must also be cautious about the uses they make of the privileged information they have on recordings or in observation notes. The ethical counselor explains honestly to parents why recordings are needed, and the writer's experience is that the only reasons that make sense to many parents are student training, research, or later use by parents. The counselor must then use the tapes only in the ways that have been promised.

In introducing the subject of tape recording, the counselor can make a simple statement such as, "I am going to record these sessions so that I [or my students and I] may learn from reviewing what we did. You may hear the tapes if you like. No one else will use them, and they will be erased at the end of the session [or semester]."

There are occasions when counselors must make notes during their sessions with parents. For example, it may be necessary to complete a case history or to note the names of participants beginning a parents' group. Generally, however, counselors should not make notes during their meetings with parents. Note-taking interrupts the natural flow of conversation. Both Garrett (1942) and Benjamin (1974) advised counselors to keep note-taking to an absolute minimum and to make notes immediately following their sessions with clients. Counselors who establish the pattern of making notes right after seeing parents will find that they will remember the important points of their conversations.

When it is necessary to make notes in the presence of parents, counselors should explain why they need to do so. Again, a brief and honest explanation will suffice.

Parenthetically, if sessions are to be taped, the recorder should be located in a place that is as inconspicuous as possible. Usually a recorder cannot be completely hidden from view; but if the counselor does not continue to call the tape recorder to parents' attention, they become engrossed in their conversations and tend to forget about it.

Adjunctive activities in many parent programs include parental observation of, or practice in, the use of certain training procedures with children. If a parent is to be engaged in such activities, this fact should be mentioned as part of the contract.

In some programs there is a fee for parental participation in counseling. In other programs there is no charge for counseling, and in others (Todd & Gottlieb, 1976), parents may receive small rewards for participation. If a fee or an incentive is a factor in a program, it should be so stated.

There is a more subtle factor counselors reveal in stating the contract: They reveal their attitudes along with explaining content. This factor is mentioned here under the heading of *What Are We Going to Do?* although it might be as appropriate to have a section titled, *What Is Our Purpose?* Counselors will decide, and so state or imply in the contract, the primary focus of forthcoming discussions and activities. In preparing to deliver congruent messages, counselors should ask themselves questions like the three below.

1. Will I insist that we talk almost exclusively about the child, or will I insist that we discuss only the parent, or can we discuss both?
2. Will I focus only on problem areas, or will I also encourage discussion of various positive aspects of life?
3. Are there topics I want to be sure that we discuss, or will I respond only to those topics suggested by a parent?

The answers to these questions indicate the counselor's position as being relatively more child-centered or more parent-centered, relatively more interested in problems or more interested in whatever the parent brings, and relatively more active or more laissez faire participants.

SAMPLE CONTRACTS

Remembering that verbalizing the contract should not occupy the entire first interview, the four examples that follow show how the counselor can combine statements about the basic elements of the contract and move on to other topics. These excerpts were taken from tapes of first interviews. C is the counselor.

1. C: We have started this weekly discussion group for mothers of children who are in the therapy program because we think you should have a chance to talk about issues in managing these children, to share information and ideas with each other and with the staff, and to feel that there is a group of people supporting your efforts. We will meet each Wednesday for eight meetings. We'll start at 1:30 and stop at 2:20 so that you can be ready to meet your children when they come out of therapy. As we meet together, I expect that we will all bring our ideas, questions, and success stories, and that we will all learn from each other.

    Probably our first job today is to get acquainted. I am going to take notes today so that I can try to associate your names and those of your children more quickly. [Turning to a mother] I know your name is Mrs. Baxter; please tell us more about you and your child and any concerns you want to be sure this group discusses.

2. C: When Mrs. Franklin [a teacher] made this appointment for us to meet together for this hour, she said you were concerned about the time Randy spends with his father. Is this what is on your mind today?

3. C: As you know we have done a lot of tests on Randy. The results are all together now and we have this hour to discuss our findings and how these square with what you see at home. Also, Dr. Goldman [a pediatrician] will come in for the last half hour, and he can answer your questions about the medical findings. If there is an area of greatest concern to you, we can start with that one and go on from there.

4. C: We have only half an hour today and I could go on for a longer time because I'm so pleased with Tim's progress in reading. I'd like to start by telling you some of the major areas of progress, and when you have things to add or have questions, please bring them up.

LIVING OUT THE CONTRACT

Counselors should be aware that all they say is not necessarily heard or understood. Despite their best efforts to offer the essentials of a contract simply and understandably, counselors will find that occasionally they will need to repeat certain contractual elements. This is neither the counselor's nor the parent's fault. As has been pointed out, each person sends and receives messages differently at different times, and each will understand some things at one time and not at others. Rather than feeling dismayed when it is necessary to re-explain a factor, counselors might feel grateful to have the chance to amend a message or to dissolve misunderstanding.

As counselors plan their contracts, they will first want to clarify their attitudes and assumptions about what should happen in their interaction with parents. When counselors have clarified their thinking, they will verbalize contracts that are more congruent with what really will transpire in their sessions.

This writer thinks that once counselors have entered into a contract with parents, they are responsible for adhering to the structure and limits they have set both for themselves and for others. If conditions dictate a change in the specified structure, the change should be explained and adequate reasons given. In this case perhaps one can think of the old contract as null and void, and a new contract can be prepared to replace it.

SUMMARY

It seems that counselors help both themselves and parents to feel a sense of order and security and to define their freedom by structuring the limitations to be placed on their interaction. The provisions of such structure is analogous to entering into a contract. Although many variables could be included in any contract, the ones the writer considers essential were discussed.

STUDY GUIDES FOR CHAPTER 5

Additional Readings

Benjamin, A. *The helping interview* (2nd ed.). Boston: Houghton-Mifflin, 1974, chapter 2.

Practice Exercises

Both of these activities can be done by people working in a group or by a person working alone. In either case there seem to be benefits to saying the statements aloud rather than writing them or just saying them to yourself.

1. Analyze each of the sample contracts on pages 58 and 59, with particular attention to the following.
   A. Is each of the basic elements discussed in the chapter included? If not, what is left out, and how might you include it?
   B. Where in each contract might the counselor pause to acknowledge a parent's questions or statements?
   C. If you were the parent to whom the counselor spoke in each example, what else would you like to know? Add whatever you like, then read aloud the entire contract as the counselor might say it.
2. Imagine three different situations, each with different conditions, in which you are the counselor seeing a parent or group of parents for the first time. Decide on your contract in view of the conditions you imagine yourself to be working with, and taking into account your answers to the questions on page 58. Make notes about each contract, but do not try to memorize it or you may lose your conversational spontaneity. Continue this activity until you are relatively comfortable with the way you verbalized these three contracts.

6

Serving As Group Leader

It is useful to think of the work of parent counselors as group leadership, with the smallest group numbering two—one counselor and one parent. To put it another way, parent counseling cannot be done by a counselor acting alone; it is necessary to have at least one other person with whom to communicate. A situation in which there is one counselor and one parent is defined here as a group. Of course group size ranges upward from the basic two.

Each person who participates in a situation contributes stimuli that affect every other person. Thus the more persons that are involved, the more elaborate will be the network of stimuli impinging on every other person. However the basic ingredients of communication are the same whether two people or several people interact. Likewise, the principles governing a counselor's behavior can remain the same no matter how many people are involved in a situation. For example, a counselor who listens to understand can practice this behavior in a session involving one parent or a dozen.

Because the same basic principles can underlie all counselor behavior and because by definition parent counseling involves at least two people, it is not very useful to dichotomize counselor–parent interactions with terms such as *individual sessions* and *group sessions*. It is more useful to think of all parent counseling as group interaction, and to use Backus's (1957) terms *two-person* and *multi-person* to indicate whether the group contains one parent or several.

The task of an effective group leader is, as Gordon (1965) pointed out, to relinquish leadership. That is, the counselor encourages each parent to assume leadership of the group. The counselor leads in creating opportunities for each person to participate verbally, to suggest discussion topics or group activities, and to pursue topics of interest—in short, the counselor helps others to direct or lead the group.

GROUPING OF PARENTS

Counselors are sometimes faced with the decision of whether to see a given parent in a two-person or a multiperson group. There is no rule on which to base such a decision; some parents seem to need one type, some need the other, and some seem to thrive in either. However, there are certain considerations that can enter into the decision.

Economy of counselor time is not the primary reason for multiperson grouping of parents. A more important rationale for the decision to see several parents in one group is based on first the fact that there are similarities among all parents; those whose children have handicaps share many of the same concerns, aspirations, ideas, and emotions as all other parents. If it is the business of counseling to help parents to deal with these aspects of their lives, as this writer believes it must be, then it can be quite beneficial to group one parent with others. Through interaction with other parents, each may feel less alone, realizing that others cope with similar problems and share similar feelings of frustration or success. Furthermore, parents learn a great deal from each other, sometimes more than they learn from counselors. Opportunity for parental learning is another reason that many counselors want to offer opportunities for multiperson interaction.

Because of parental similarities, it is quite possible, often desirable, to have groups contain parents of children of somewhat different ages and/or with different disorders. For example, this writer's groups often include parents of children with language disorders, children with articulation disorders, and children with hearing or motor impairments affecting both speech and language. Similarities between parents are not created exclusively by their children's disorders. Neither are parental uniquenesses created by their children. Thus it becomes possible to help parents deal with similar life issues, to cope with their individual concerns, and to develop their uniquely creative ways of behaving through interaction with those of diverse experience.

There is, of course, an upper limit to how different parents can be in their interests and backgrounds if they are to enjoy working together and if they are to work productively. For example, parents of high school children are at a different place from the parents of preschool children; mixing such parents in one group is usually inadvisable unless the counselor can find other bases on which their relationship can be sustained.

Counselor caution is also advisable when mixing parents of widely divergent educational or socioeconomic backgrounds. It is quite possible to group such parents, however, if the counselor is aware of the potential threat felt by the less educated or advantaged, and if the counselor helps each parent respect and build on his or her unique strengths and positive attributes. There are attributes that are more important in human relations than education or socioeconomic status. Sometimes the counselor's attitudes of respect and appreciation can be implemented by others and the group functions well; sometimes a very disparate group just doesn't work. Among the many possible examples of groups that didn't seem to jell and those that did, a successful example is pleasant to consider.

A woman (Mrs. A) with an eighth-grade education attended a group with three other mothers, one of whom held an advanced degree in engineering (Mrs. B), one of whom lived on a farm and who had not completed high school (Mrs. C), and one who had a high school degree. The group was scheduled to meet for an hour weekly for 6 weeks.

After the second meeting, during which Mrs. B had talked a great deal and used an elaborate vocabulary and Mrs. A had silently scowled a great deal, Mrs. A approached the counselor. She complained, "Mrs. B uses such big words I can't understand a thing she's saying, but I just know she's looking down her nose at me." The counselor elected not to discuss this matter at length with only Mrs. A and said, "I'd like others to know how you feel too. Would you be able to say this in the group next week?" Mrs. A said she would try.

The following week, the counselor started the group dis-

cussion by saying, "I think Mrs. A has had some feelings about
this group, and I have encouraged her to express them directly
to you." Mrs. A spoke up, "Mainly I feel like I just can't follow
you [looking at Mrs. B]. You know, I didn't even get to ninth
grade before I married." Mrs. B looked surprised. Mrs. C
volunteered, "I know what you mean. I don't know where you
learned all those big words [looking at Mrs. B] and I thought last
week [turning to Mrs. A], I'm just a farm girl and I can't talk
like that and don't want to. But you know, if you can listen all
the way to the end of a sentence, she usually says something
worth listening to." Mrs. B protested that, "I really didn't want
to come off like that. I guess I'm just so glad to get a chance to
talk over these things, but I don't want to do that. Please tell me
if I'm sounding stuffy again." The counselor said to the group,
"I think Mrs. B really wants your help just as you want to be
understood by her. I suggest we think about starting over, like
this is a new day, because I feel a real spirit here of all of us
wanting to be on friendly terms. Would it perhaps help us if we
called each other by our first names?" Group members thought
that perhaps it would.

The upshort of the incident was that Mrs. B did learn to
modify her verbal behavior, adjusting both the amount she
talked and the vocabulary she used, with the help of the counselor and other parents. The counselor served as a model of one
who did not hesitate to ask Mrs. B to clarify statements that
were unclear, occasionally asking her, "Is this what you
mean," then restating her words. The other mothers helped
Mrs. B too, in their own unique ways. For example, at one
meeting Mrs. C said to her, "Oops, slow it down [using Mrs.
B's first name]. I'm lost and I don't want to be."

Although not all-important, another consideration in grouping
of parents is related to the children's disorders. When the unique
problems created by a certain type of disorder are likely to occupy a
great deal of a group's attention, it usually is wise to form a group
with parents whose children have that same disorder. For example,
the needs of parents of deaf infants, who must learn how to develop
communication with their children, are of such magnitude that they
justify forming a group exclusively for them. Counselors should
remember, however, that such a group is by no means homoge-

neous. Where there are two parents, there is a heterogeneous group. Although sharing similar concerns, each parent is a unique individual, and counselors should expect that each one will react differently.

Notwithstanding the fact that multiperson groups can benefit parents by offering support and helping them both to clarify issues and to experiment with new ideas and behaviors, certain conditions should lead a counselor to recommend two-person counseling for a given parent. One such condition is the number of parents available to meet at a given time. For example, in many clinics initial diagnostic interviews are done with one parent or with the family of one child, and that is the only such interview taking place at the time.

Parental difficulty with the mechanics of communication may indicate a need for two-person grouping. I elected, for example, to see a woman with a severe articulation disorder in a two-person situation in an attempt to avoid further complicating the parent–counselor communication. A similar decision was made when the deaf parents of a preschool child requested counseling. (These deaf persons actually were seen in a four-person group; an interpreter served the vital function of transmitting counselor's and parents' communications through signs.)

There are other parents who need more attention focused on them, at least for a time, than would be possible if other parents shared the time. This is not to say such parents are emotionally disturbed or have pathologic problems. Some such parents must make unique decisions in a short period of time, so they need help in clarifying issues relatively quickly. For example, during a summer session a woman asked for time alone with a counselor. She felt she needed to get her thoughts together in order to decide about her son's school placement in the fall, and the decision had to be made in 2 weeks.

Other parents find it very frightening to share ideas or emotions. The counselor must judge in each case whether placing such a person with other parents would be so overwhelming as to outweigh its benefits. A word of caution is in order here, because many persons verbalize fear of talking in groups. A counselor should listen to more of what parents say about this fear, rather than taking it at face value.

I use various models of grouping. Some parents are seen exclusively in multiparent groups, others have all of their counseling experience alone with the counselor. Some parents begin their work with one or several two-person visits, followed by a series of sessions that include other parents. For other parents the process is reversed; they begin work in a multiparent group, followed by one or several sessions alone with the counselor. In keeping with attitudes of respect, it is also obvious that when there is a choice, parents should participate in the decision about which type of situation seems to be in their best interests.

FACILITATING GROUP DISCUSSION

Discussion is the chief medium utilized in parent counseling. It can occupy participants for an entire session or it can precede or follow other activities. This writer prefers to engage in informal discussion. Topics to be considered can be suggested either by the counselor or by a parent. The topic can be very specific. For example, a mother may wish to discuss how to help her child adjust to his leg braces, or a counselor may suggest such a topic. Topics can also be general ones such as discipline, adjustment of children to their peers, or ways of communicating with children.

Seating Arrangements

Informal discussion is facilitated by meeting in a room with comfortable furniture arranged so that participants can see each other. Such rooms are not always available, however, and many counselors must adapt space to their use.

Remembering that people should be able to see those with whom they communicate and that artificial barriers should not come between them, various types of rooms can be utilized. For example, an office, classroom, or auditorium can be equipped with chairs arranged in a circle, utilizing all or only part of the available space.

The size of the meeting room will necessarily limit the size of the groups. For example, the writer does much of her work with parents in her office, which necessarily limits groups to not more than six participants.

As Benjamin (1974) cautioned, counselors should pay attention to where they sit; he particularly warned that sitting behind a desk can suggest an attitude of authority or desire to teach. When a counselor sits just outside the group's circle, it can signal withdrawal or discomfort.

Giving Each Person a Chance to Talk

It is relatively easy to provide equal opportunities for participation in a two-person situation in which a counselor must keep in touch with the needs of only one parent. The multiperson group offers a greater challenge for the counselor who wishes to provide equal opportunities within the formal or informal discussion. It is uncomfortable to all to have a situation in which two persons talk at great length while other group members merely wait their turn and are not included as discussants. Counselors cannot insure absolute equality in talking time, nor should they try to do so lest they violate an individual's need to participate silently. But counselors can avoid engaging in a series of two-person conversations under the guise of a multiperson situation.

Tape recording the sessions and counting and timing the participants' verbalizations can help counselors correct gross inequalities. For example, one counselor was amazed to learn that in a 45-minute session with four parents, Mr. A spoke four times for a total of 22 minutes, Mrs. B spoke three times for a total of 8 minutes, the counselor's eight verbalizations occupied 7 minutes, Mrs. C had four verbalizations for 7 minutes, and Mrs. D spoke three times for a total of 1 minute.

When parents do not have relatively equal chances to participate, it can become disturbing to all. Parents may become bored, restless, and irritated. When given a choice, they may elect not to return if there are subsequent sessions. The counselor in such a group is likely to feel frustration. Because of the advantages of multiperson participation for many parents, counselors will want to utilize various means to help create an atmosphere in which each parent is given a relatively equal opportunity to participate in ways that are valued, respected, and reinforced.

It may be necessary for a counselor to insist that parents take turns in a multiperson group. When parents have to vie with each other for a chance to talk or when one parent is permitted to dominate the conversation, the total group is likely to disintegrate into several subgroups, all perhaps talking at once. Counselors should find tactfully direct ways to prevent such confusion. For example, the writer often makes a statement such as, "Wait, Mrs. B, it's Mrs. C's turn to talk. We'll come back to your point in a minute." When the counselor hushes one parent in such fashion, it is imperative that the counselor see to it that the parent has a chance to participate verbally as promised. Again, when two people have started a side discussion that does not include others in the group, this writer has said something like, "Mrs. B and Mrs. C, I'd like all of us to hear your ideas. Would you share them with all of us?" The intent is not to embarrass or punish parents. Rather, the writer intends to head off possible embarrassment or punishment meted out later by her or by other parents because of the disruptive behavior.

Recognizing Similarities Between Parents

Counselors can facilitate discussion in multiperson situations by pointing out similarities between parents. Again, it is not necessary for the parents to have had any of the same experiences; similarities are to be found in their ideas, attitudes, and emotions. The following example illustrates several ways that counselors can point out parental similarities.

> Mrs. B talked on one occasion about her frustration with her son Matthew's reluctance to play with other children and her reluctance to encourage him to seek out his peers. Mrs. B said, "I know children have teased him before, and I sure don't want to push him into situations that set him up for teasing." The counselor said, "Sure, you don't want to make it harder for him, and being with other kids could be both good and hard for him. Perhaps some of the rest of you [looking at other parents] know what it feels like to be in a bind, not knowing what's best to do for your children."

Here the counselor's leading statement opened an opportunity for any of the parents to respond; leading statements are open-ended and invite discussion. In this situation the counselor invited participation but did not direct the invitation to any particular person. This counselor was satisfied that all could feel included in her gaze. Such visual inclusion, coupled with a leading statement, often is enough to help parents feel that they are participating.

Had the counselor wished to be more certain of eliciting a verbal response, she might have added a general question such as, "Who catches the kind of feeling she is expressing?" Or the counselor might have asked for a response from a specific participant by adding a direct question such as, "Mrs. A, perhaps you have felt the kind of feeling she is expressing?" or "What about you, Mrs. A, can you remember an instance of feeling like she says she does?"

The counselor in the above example also had the option of asking other parents to give Mrs. B some suggestions. The request for parental suggestions could have been imbedded within a context of acknowledging and using parental similarities. For example, the counselor could have added a general question such as, "From your experience of feeling like you weren't quite sure what was best, what suggestions can you give Mrs. B?" Again, such an open-ended question can be asked directly of one of the other parents.

Counselor options are numerous. The important point is that counselors can respect and utilize parental similarities to promote interaction.

Responding to Visual Cues

In a multiperson group the counselor needs to have all participants within visual range. People give signals that indicate their wish to talk or their wish to remain silent. Visual cues expressing a willingness to talk include sitting forward in the chair, nodding the head affirmatively, or opening the mouth as if to speak. As a counselor glimpses such an indication of a parent's willingness to talk, it is usually safe to ask the parent to do so. For example, during a discussion, Mrs. C, who had been silent, began to frown and nod. When one person finished speaking, the counselor said, "Mrs. C, you look as if you had something to add." Mrs. C then spoke of her ideas, thereby participating in a way she had not done previously in the session.

Using Plural Pronouns

Counselors' use of plural pronouns when conversing in multiperson groups will promote group interaction. It is fairly easy to substitute plural for singular pronouns. For example, rather than saying "Tell me more about that," the counselor can say "Tell us more about that,'' or ''We'd like to hear more about that.'' The use of a plural pronoun acknowledges the presence of more than one listener, includes more than one parent in the counselor's comments, and thus encourages more than one to participate. Because of the potential benefits, counselors are encouraged to practice using more plural pronouns and fewer singular ones when interacting in multiperson groups.

Selecting Topics for Discussion

Counselors help parents participate by asking them to suggest topics of interest to them. Some parents are very eager to suggest topics for group discussion; others are more hesitant. Some parents who seem reluctant to help plan the group's discussion are quite zealous in helping the group pursue a discussion topic once it has been suggested.

The counselor should also contribute topics. Earlier (1966; 1968) I suggested that parents might profitably discuss several *tools* for promoting parent–child communication. Among these tools was listening to understand, the assumption being that just as it is helpful to parents to talk with those who listen to them, it might also be helpful to them to listen to their children in this way. Usually the counselor is the one who suggests such topics as listening, because early in their counseling experience many parents do not visualize the need for discussing such ideas.

Some counselors seem reluctant to suggest topics to parents, perhaps fearing that parents will not be interested or will resent the counselor's ideas. It is unfortunate when counselors are hesitant to raise topics they consider important because their failure to do so may prevent parental access to those ideas. The suggestion to such counselors is that they view themselves as group participants with equal rights to raise and try to pursue ideas. If their ideas do not meet parental needs, parents will so indicate.

Providing for Silence

Although this section has emphasized ways of helping parents to participate verbally, counselors should not take this to mean that only parental verbalization is valued. Counselors should not overvalue talking and overlook the benefits of silence. As the previous chapter points out, silence can be as productive, often more productive, than speaking.

When parents give signs of needing not to participate verbally, counselors should respect their needs and really grant them the right to be quiet. At such times counselors may find it useful to remind themselves that parent discussion groups exist for the purpose of giving parents an opportunity to engage in discussion *if they choose to do so.*

ROLEPLAYING

Although discussion remains the primary medium for parent counseling, roleplaying offers a viable alternative. By definition, roleplaying is the acting out or demonstrating of situations. Discussion is an integral part of roleplaying, and often situations to be enacted are suggested as people converse. But roleplaying goes beyond merely talking about a situation or event. As Wolpe (1957) pointed out, roleplaying provides greater opportunities than discussion does for emotional as well as cognitive involvement, and Corsini (1966) noted that through roleplaying participants can demonstrate behaviors that arise from various attitudes, ideas and emotions. Corsini, Shaw, and Blake (1961) also cited the value of roleplaying as a tool for teaching new behaviors.

Because of the greater number of potential role-takers, roleplaying may be more easily used in multiperson than in two-person groups. However it can be useful in two-person situations. For example, a mother stated that her son, Terry, did not know how to play with other children, that he was selfish and demanding. The counselor said, "Let's imagine I'm another child and I've brought some toys over and want to play with Terry. You be Terry and show what he might do that's selfish and demanding." The mother demonstrated her son's behavior. Following her enactment of what she had seen Terry do, the parent–counselor discussion continued.

The above example raises a matter that counselors should consider. The term *roleplaying* frightens some parents, who feel they must be skilled actors if they are to participate. Counselors of course set no such standards, as there is no right or wrong way to enact any role. In the absence of high counselor requirements for acting skill, it is probably the term itself that stirs parental feelings of being on the spot or being the focus of attention, thus activating their reluctance to participate. Counselors need not use the term *roleplaying;* they can refer instead to the processes involved—showing and imagining or pretending.

Similarly, this writer has learned not to ask a parent to roleplay with such an invitation as, "Would you like to show what Terry does?" Such a question may invite a response of "No." An invitation like the one issued by the counselor in the above example more often insures parental participation. The counselor can make such a request in a context revealing his appreciation that the parent may not view such demonstration as useful. Thus the counselor can grant, but not invite, the parent's refusal.

Counselors should also remember that in a multiperson group, all parents need not participate in role enactment to benefit from the procedure. Often those who have not played roles are active in the discussion following roleplaying; thus they participate in a way that is comfortable to them. Other parents have reported that although they felt unable to engage in this process, they felt they learned from watching others play roles.

Selecting Situations for Roleplaying

Situations that lend themselves to roleplaying can arise from discussion. Either the counselor or a parent can suggest that such situations be demonstrated, although usually it is the counselor who does so. The counselor also can introduce roleplaying without prior discussion. In considering *what* to roleplay, counselors must first consider *why* they use this procedure.

Roleplaying is useful for teaching a new behavior. Whenever the counselor asks a parent to learn a new skill, it is useful to demonstrate the behavior. For example, the counselor asked Mrs. J to help her son, Johnny, with his speech notebook. The counselor played Mrs. J and Mrs. J took the role of her son. In this way the counselor showed Mrs. J what she was being asked to do.

Situations that require parents to choose between several behaviors lend themselves to roleplaying. Three examples follow.

Mrs. M reported that her 6-year-old son, Matthew, hated to get up in the morning and was often late for school. Mrs. M characterized school mornings as "sheer chaos" as she frantically tried to get the boy up and off, tried to get breakfast for Matthew and her husband (who got angry when she called Matthew several times and he still did not appear), tried to get her husband off to work, and tried to get herself ready in case she had to drive Matthew to school to prevent his being late. Mrs. M had tried setting the alarm for Matthew, had spanked him when he did not come when called for breakfast, and had made him stay in the house after school on days when he was late. Other alternatives were suggested by other parents in Mrs. M's group, and several of the choices were roleplayed.

Mr. C wondered what to do when his son "sassed" him. Another father in the group asked Mr. C to show what the boy did that was sassy. Mr. C played the son and the other man played Mr. C. Following this roleplaying, group members suggested several choices Mr. C might make in responding to his son's behavior. The choice Mr. C said he preferred was roleplayed.

Following a teacher's classroom demonstration of a behavior modification procedure to be used by Mrs. L, Mrs. L asked the counselor, "What if my child doesn't react like that child in the demonstration did?" Mrs. L described how she thought her child might react. The counselor then assumed the child's role and Mrs. L experimented with several ways she might behave if her child did react in ways she had predicted.

Emotional involvement is an aspect of all roleplaying, but this procedure can be used with the express purpose of helping people express pent-up emotions. For example, Mrs. B had spoken of her extreme anger toward her sister, who had told Mrs. B's child that she was retarded, spoiled, and going nowhere because "You're so lazy!" Mrs. B said she had a hard time expressing any anger and the counselor said, "Well, I'm not your sister but let's pretend I am. You can safely say to me what you'd like to say to her." Mrs. B agreed, and the counselor asked, "Do you want me to fight back?" Mrs. B exclaimed, "Oh, please do! I'll think of so many things to be mad about." After a heated exchange, Mrs. B said, "Whew, I feel better! I really let you have it! Now I can talk about how I'm going to handle it the next time she comes out with these things to Jennifer [her daughter]."

An example of using roleplaying to help a person express warm positive emotions occurred when Mrs. J reported that her son, Terry, had made her a valentine. His presentation of the loving gift so touched her that she didn't know what to say, "though I wanted to let him know how much it meant to me." The counselor suggested that another woman in the group play Terry and that Mrs. J tell the roleplayed version of Terry what she would like to say to her son. The two played the scene. The following day Mrs. J stopped the counselor in the hall to report that she had been able to express her pleasure about the valentine to her satisfaction and that Terry had said, "Gee, Mom, I thought you'd really love it and I'm glad you finally said so."

In Mrs. J's case it is possible to infer that application had been made of the experience of roleplaying an emotion; often there is no such immediate evidence. This writer thinks there is value in the exercise of roleplayed emotion for its release of feelings that may be locked up, whether or not parents report direct application of such freedom.

Conducting Roleplaying

The same counselor behaviors that encourage parents to function as discussants are used to help them to take part in roleplaying. Counselors should arrange seating so that all group members can see each other; here again, participants will rely on visual cues. Counselors should give each parent a chance to participate in some way, either by taking a role or within the discussion that is part of the roleplaying process. But again, the counselor should not insist on verbal participation.

When counselors conduct roleplaying, it is preferable that they lead or direct the activity and not participate by playing a role. The reason for this preference is the difficulty in attending closely to two things—leading and creating a role—at the same time. Of course it is necessary that the counselor play a role in a two-person group. It is much easier both to direct and to participate in a two-person situation, because it is more simplified than one in which there may be four or five roles to keep up with.

Because roleplaying is a fluid process, it is often difficult to differentiate one phase of the process from another, but essentially there are three stages: warm-up, acting out the roles, and discussion.

WARM-UP

The warm-up period is whatever time it takes to set up the situation, to select roles, and to help participants begin to create the roles they will play. The amount of warm-up that is necessary varies greatly. For example, a mother playing her own child can probably create the role much more easily than a young father playing his grandmother. Several of the preceding examples illustrate the playing of one's own child. The following excerpts indicate how warm-up was accomplished in the case of a 26-year-old man (B) playing his 82-year-old grandmother. The counselor (C) conducted the warm-up.

C: You're visiting your grandson, Mrs. B?
B: Yes, he's my youngest grandson.
C: You sound like you're really fond of him. Right?
B: You bet I am . . . apple of my eye. It's fun to visit him . . . different from home. She's all alone there, you know.
C: [ignoring the third person reference] Oh, you live alone?
B: Yep, and I don't want to live with any of my kids . . . . It gets awfully lonely . . . . My daughter is close by . . . but no kids around at home, and B has kids.
C: You like your grandson's kids?
B: Mercy yes, I like everything about B! His kids are live wires— so bad! But they make me feel young . . . . I love those kids . . . don't feel old when they're around.

Acting Out Roles

When all those to play roles have gotten a feeling for the situation and their parts in it, the action begins. Often it happens that a person interrupts the action to ask for more warm-up. For example, a man playing a neighbor gossiping about the family of a handicapped child, interrupted his conversation with another "neighbor" to say, "Hey, I forgot why I don't like your family." When the woman who had asked that the scene be role played supplied the man with his reason, the action continued. Such breaks are necessary and useful; it is not useful to interrupt the action for the sake of discussing what went on in the scene.

Discussion

When acting out the scene has ended, discussion of it can begin. All participants, both those who have played roles and those who have watched, have a chance to discuss aspects such as what they thought or felt about the situation, why a role was played a certain way, and how the roles might have been played differently.

Discussants may suggest that roles be changed and the scene replayed. They may suggest new situations to be enacted. In these cases either the discussion or the previous action may provide all the warm-up necessary. For example, a woman said, "I saw how you played that kid and you saw how I handled your temper tantrum; now I'll play the kid and you handle this fit I'm about to fling." The two began immediately to play the revised scene.

SUMMARY

A discussion format is the one primarily used in two-person and multiperson parent counseling. Roleplaying offers a valuable alternative to the exclusive use of discussion. Other vehicles for counselor–parent interaction can suggest themselves to counselors, or can be suggested by parents, such as those described by Murphy (1976).

Effective group leaders are those who relinquish leadership. Various means were discussed by which counselors can help parents to participate and to assume leadership. The effective leader respects the rights and utilizes the abilities of others. Perhaps counselors can assess improvement in their group leadership by noting their greater willingness to be led by parents as well as to lead them.

STUDY GUIDES FOR CHAPTER 6

Additional Readings

Corsini, R. *Roleplaying in psychotherapy: A manual.* Chicago: Aldine, 1966, chaps. 1, 2, 3, 7.
Gordon, T. Group-centered leadership and administration. In C. Rogers (ed.)., *Client-centered therapy* (paperback ed.). Boston: Houghton-Mifflin, 1965, chap. 8.
Webster, E. Procedures for group parent counseling in speech pathology and audiology. *Journal of Speech and Hearing Disorders,* 1968, *33:* 127–131.

Practice Exercises

1. List several visual cues a peson can use to indicate willingness to partic-ipate in a group's activity. These cues should be ones that can be given without verbalization and should not duplicate those listed in this chapter.
2. Sit quietly during a multiperson conversation. While listening to other persons, try also to think of what things others in the group could do to help *you* enter the conversation.
3. Review the possible uses of silence that were discussed in Chapter 4. Then listen to a conversation between two or more people. Sit quietly and make hunches about the ways each person who is *not* talking may be using silence.
4. As leader, set up a roleplaying situation, leading participants through all the stages of this activity. One experience will not make you a comfortable leader, so it is suggested that you practice leading such roleplaying activities until you do feel more comfortable with the process.

7

Terminating A Session or Series of Sessions

Because both counselors and parents must have a sense of order and structure, it is important that all parties know the point at which their meeting ends, and have the chance to experience closure at that point. Counselors need to consider various ways to close a single session because the optimum way to close one interview can serve as the model for termination of a series of sessions.

Counselors can help parents to prepare for termination from the very beginning of their interaction. That is, to the extent that a counselor demonstrates respect for a parent's ability to chart his own course, helps the parent talk about and clarify ideas and feelings upon which action will be based, and helps the parent think about and experiment with new behaviors, the counselor is helping the parent to function independently. Such parental independence will be necessary when the session with the counselor is over.

A counselor also helps a parent to prepare for termination when the counselor–parent contract is stated. When the counselor explains the time limitations for a session or series of sessions, a parent can then adjust to a definite time segment after which such interaction will cease.

On the other hand, the time to terminate a single session may come as a surprise to both counselor and parent. If either one is absorbed in sharing an experience, neither may be inclined to think

81

about, or to plan for, terminating their interaction. To the extent that either is deeply involved in interaction in the present, it is *right now* that is important, and thoughts of *afterwards* may have little relevance. The state of being absorbed in the present situation is a common one. Many persons have had the experience of being so deeply engrossed in a conversation, book, or movie, that they simply lost track of time or forgot what they had planned to do afterwards.

Total absorption in the present is desirable. Nevertheless, counseling sessions do have to end. Part of the counselor–parent contract concerns *when* the sessions(s) will end. In addition, the counselor should have in mind *how* each session and a series of sessions will end.

Some counselors like to summarize the topics discussed in a session as a way to provide closure. While respecting those who can terminate by summarizing, I usually do not try to do so, except when a task-oriented group has met to solve a specific problem or plan a specific course of action. In other counseling sessions I seem to do a poor job of summarizing. Part of the reason for stumbling, perhaps, is awareness that one can capture only the essence of the content discussed, but that the meanings expressed are much more elusive and cannot be summarized adequately. Another reason for reluctance to summarize arises from the suspicion that one may miss hearing something of importance while formulating and delivering the summary. In other words, while trying to say what has happened in the previous period of time, the counselor may miss something else of equal importance.

However the counselor chooses to end a session, it is the counselor who provides the model for termination. In planning how to terminate a session with parents, the counselor should assume responsibility in three areas: (a) adhering to time limitations, (b) closing on a relatively positive note, and (c) avoiding promises that cannot be kept.

ADHERING TO TIME LIMITS

After saying that counselors should actively listen to parents and that both counselors and parents can momentarily lose all sense of time, it may sound incongruous to say that counselors need to be aware of time limitations. This statement is not as paradoxical as it may sound because of two factors.

First, human beings are time-bound creatures. They adjust so thoroughly to the constraints of time that they may seem equipped with built-in clocks. This adjustment to time can be troublesome when it causes jet-lag after a flight from New York to Los Angeles, or when it prompts the baby to cry at 2 a.m. when a mother's built-in clock says it's time to sleep. Such time-boundedness can be helpful when it makes either a counselor or parent become aware of the passage of time. As the counselor or parent senses that "our time together is almost over," one or the other probably will look at a watch or clock. This interruption of the flow of conversation between them arises from inner stimuli and cannot be prevented. The interruption becomes a major distraction only if one attempts to ignore it. If one acknowledges the inner prompting that time is passing and checks on the time remaining, the distraction passes and the conversation can be picked up at the point where it was interrupted. When used in this way, one's inner clock is useful in keeping track of the time to insure external order.

A second factor assists counselors who wish to keep track of the time: No conversation can run on without the participants' pausing for breath now and again; in short, there will always be pauses in the conversation. These pauses, coupled with the counselor's sense that time is passing, provide places where the counselor can check on the amount of time remaining. This process is analogous to what one does while watching a football game: One is less likely to look at one's watch while the quarterback is passing for a touchdown; one is more likely to consult the watch while the teams pause and return to their huddles. One's tendency to use a break in the action of a football game to check the amount of time remaining is in no way disrespectful of the gladiators on the field, nor is it evidence of one's lack of interest in the game. It is a way one can acknowledge one's inner prompting about time and can do something to orient oneself to the time remaining. The writer believes this time consciousness is necessary in counseling. In no way should a counselor feel apologetic for being aware of time, nor should he try to keep track of time surreptitiously. When counselors openly and honestly keep up with the time, they live out willingness to accept their share of responsibility for this important aspect of structure.

It has already been mentioned that initially the counselor assumes the major share of responsibility for time keeping. But because parents also have built-in clocks, they will come to share this responsibility. Indeed, many parents not only keep track of time but also seem to want to initiate the termination process. This parental need should be acknowledged and utilized. Beginning counselors sometimes construe a parent's need to initiate the ending of a session as evidence of that parent's boredom, lack of interest, resistance, or some such negative state. This parental need is not necessarily negative. When a parent initiates the termination of a session, it may indicate the need to be active or to behave independently, both of which seem to be positive states. Thus, although counselors set the model for adjusting to the time limits of sessions, they can count on the fact that each participant will come to share the responsibility for time-keeping.

Ending a session *comfortably* on time is also important in maintaining the flow of open, productive communication between counselor and parent. Consider the following example between a mother, P, and a counselor, C.

P: My husband thinks I'm silly to worry so much.
C: What makes you feel that he does?
P: You know what he said in front of his mother about my "bucket of silly worries about Tim." That really hurt me.
C: It hurt and you felt angry.
P: Oh yes, I was angry! I wanted to slap his face! I just wanted to scream at him at the top of my lungs . . . .
C: What did you feel like screaming at him?
P: I felt like *yelling,* "You fink, what about——"
C: Oh gosh, our time is up. We have to stop for today. [Rising and moving toward the door] We can go on with this next time if you like.

Such a scene is distressing to both counselor and parent. The parent has been encouraged to discuss her feelings, then interrupted while doing so and hastily ushered out. The counselor is no doubt embarrassed and dissatisfied with this behavior. Thus this terminal interaction can have negative meanings for both participants, and indeed it may be a stumbling block in any future encounter between them. Counselors will lose track of time now and again; it is not completely avoidable. However there are two things the counselor can do to decrease the possibility of being caught in such upsetting straits.

First, the counselor can check the time and can advise the parent of the amount of time remaining. Notification of the time can be made with short statements such as, "I see we have 5 minutes more," or "We have about 5 minutes until it's time to stop," or "I see our time is about up; we have just 5 more minutes." The writer uses 5-minute warnings because she feels comfortable notifying people that there are approximately 5 minutes remaining. There is nothing magic about 5 minutes; a counselor may feel more comfortable with an announcement when 10 or 3 remain. The important thing is to help participants set the stage for ending comfortably on time.

The second way to assist with closing is to refrain from introducing a new topic when no time remains for its discussion. However a counselor cannot prevent a parent from introducing a new topic. As Rogers (1965) pointed out, a client may introduce a subject of great importance in the closing moments of a session. When a parent introduces a topic of concern near the end of a session, the counselor does not want to inhibit parental expression on the topic, but wants to avoid any implication that unlimited discussion of the topic is possible.

While being aware of time and refraining from introducing new topics near the end of a session, the counselor can find a number of ways to listen while still terminating the session on time. The following examples illustrate two alternatives to the previous example of a counselor and an angry mother.

P: My husband thinks I'm silly to worry so much.
C: I'm aware that we have only about 2 minutes left, but I'd like to hear why you feel that way.
P: You know, what he said in front of his mother about my "bucket of silly worries about Tim." That really hurt me.
C: It really hurt your feelings for him to tell his mother that.
P: Oh yes, and was I angry! I wanted to slap his face! I wanted to scream at him at the top of my lungs!
C: Yes, hurt and anger can work together that way. Sometimes hurt feelings come out in anger, don't they?
P: Maybe I do worry a lot, but he needn't talk to his mother about it.

C: Maybe you do. We can talk more about this whole thing next time if you like, but I suggest we stop here and plan to continue our discussion next time.

P: My husband thinks I'm silly to worry so much.

C: He has said you worry too much?

P: Well, yes and no. Partly it's one more way he uses to criticize me in front of his mother.

C: Oh yes, you have some strong feelings when you think he's criticizing you in front of her.

P: You bet I do!

C: Yes, the feeling of being criticized isn't pleasant and I'm sure we could talk much more about this. I notice, though, that today we have only a minute or two left and I think we can't really explore this topic very well in such a short time. I suggest we stop here. But you can be sure we'll pick up this topic next time if you like.

There are, of course, a multitude of other alternatives that are consistent with a counselor's wish to end the session on time without the shock and confusion of suddenly having to do so.

CLOSING THE SESSION ON A RELATIVELY POSITIVE NOTE

The "feeling tone" of some topics is fairly neutral. Other topics are more emotionally loaded, carrying a strong positive or negative feeling tone. Within any one session, counselor–parent discussion is likely to move back and forth between the more neutral and more loaded topics. If, as the point of termination approaches, the topic being discussed is one that stirs strong positive feelings, the interview will end on a positive note. If, however, the topic is laden with strong negative emotions, the need to leave the session can increase parental distress. No one likes to leave an office or conference room visibly upset and shaken, perhaps struggling for control, or perhaps trying to talk rationally while feeling not the least bit rational. Anyone who has been in such a situation knows how the feeling of lack of control can compound whatever distress one feels. Rather than dismissing a parent in this state of discomfiture, the counselor can help the person to regain composure while still in the conference room.

The counselor can use various means to help a parent feel some closure on negative emotions and turn to a somewhat more positive topic before leaving. This writer prefers to state directly the intention to help a parent diminish negative feelings before leaving a session. Returning to the example of the hurt and angry woman used in the previous section of this chapter, the counselor could say something like, "I know you feel so angry about that, but you'd probably rather not be upset when you go to meet Tim. We can talk about this more next time. For now, let's talk about something a little less upsetting before you leave." The precise wording the counselor uses is less important than the intent to help the parent feel some closure and to end in a more positive vein.

This is not to imply that all final segments of a session must be filled with sweetness and light. Such a goal, if desirable, is unobtainable. It seems to the writer, however, that a counselor can share responsibility for helping a parent to leave feeling fairly composed and with a greater feeling of self-control than would be possible if the parent left while still in the process of discussing strong negative feelings.

AVOIDING PROMISES THAT CANNOT BE KEPT

In their desire to end a parent interview on a positive note and to be helpful in the future, counselors can unwittingly make promises that have a low probability of being carried out. These promises are (a) those that are situationally impossible to implement, or (b) those that would create injustice for the counselor, and therefore for the parent. One example will serve to amplify these two pitfalls.

A busy teacher reported that she ended one of her monthly meetings with parents by saying, "You can call me anytime you have a problem or question." However her daily schedule at school precluded her going to the office to answer the phone at just any time, and after arriving home she wanted to spend time relating with, and providing for, her husband and two young children. She really did not wish to have her time with her family interrupted by frequent phone calls. After several parents had in good faith accepted her invitation to call, and had unknowingly intruded on her school or home activity, she learned to say, "You can call me at school either during the half hour before school or the hour after school if you have further problems or questions."

This teacher had wanted to indicate her genuine willingness to be helpful. Her first way of expressing this desire was in terms of a promise; but her busy schedule and her need for involvement with her own family precluded her carrying out the promise. Her amended message gave parents freedom within the limitations of what was possible and desirable for both them and the teacher.

There are other promises that should be avoided or made only if conditions permit their fulfillment. "I'll be happy to see you any-time" can reflect the counselor's attitude but not necessarily his schedule. Likewise, "We can talk more about this later," is a good promise unless a parent can be seen for only one session. "I'll make an appointment for you with Dr. Jones," is also an acceptable prom-ise if it is within the counselor's province to make appointments with Dr. Jones. However the statement is erroneous, and could be perceived by the parent as a broken promise, if it is found that in fact Dr. Jones makes appointments only with those who call in person. Before stating a promise, it seems wise for counselors to assess the constraints on their ability to fulfill that which has been promised.

SUMMARY

There are many ways to terminate parent interviews. The be-haviors counselors find useful in closing one session can also be employed as they terminate a series of sessions. The important variables to be considered are adhering to the limitations of time, closing on a relatively positive theme, and avoiding promises that cannot be kept.

STUDY GUIDES FOR CHAPTER 7

Additional Readings

Benjamin, A. *The helping interview* (2nd ed.). Boston: Houghton-Mifflin, 1974, pp. 28–32.

Practice Exercises

1. Referring to the example of Tim's mother that was used in this chapter, roleplay two or three 5-minute situations in which you are the counselor. Start each situation with the woman's statement, ''My husband thinks I'm silly to worry so much.'' From there on the mother can respond to your verbalization in any way she chooses. The task of the counselor is to listen to her and to try to understand what her world is like, while ending the session comfortably on time and on a relatively positive note. Discuss each situation immediately after it has been played. Listen to what the person who played Tim's mother thought and felt about counselor behaviors as termination approached.
2. Set up three different situations in which you as counselor will practice closing a session. Keep in mind the variables of staying within the allotted time, trying to end on a positive theme, and avoiding untenable promises.
3. List several statements counselors could make in an effort to indicate willingness to be of further help to parents. Each statement should include only promises that can be carried out.

PART III

Implementing Counselor Functions

Counselors are aware of limitations on their power to help parents. It is impossible to erase all parental hurt, concern, guilt, or self condemnation. Nevertheless, counselors can provide needed help, as the word was defined by Benjamin (1974, p. XII).

Help is an enabling act. The interviewer enables the interviewee to recognize, to feel, to know, to decide, to choose whether to change. This enabling act involves giving on the part of the interviewer. He must give of his time, his capacity to listen and understand, his skill, his knowledge, his interest—part of himself. If this giving can be perceived by the interviewee, the enabling act will involve receiving. The interviewee will receive the help in a way possible for him to receive it and for it to remain meaningful to him. The helping interview is the largely verbal interaction between interviewer and interviewee in which this enabling act takes place. It takes place but does not always succeed in its purpose; often we do not know if it has or not.

Basically, counselors serve four helpful functions for parents. They receive information from parents, give information to parents, help parents clarify their ideas, attitudes, and emotions, and help parents learn new behaviors.

It is recognized that these basic functions can be separated only for purposes of discussion. In actual practice, there is no clear dividing line; that is, any given counselor utterance may serve several purposes. Although in practice the four functions are inseparable, each is discussed individually in this section.

8

Receiving Information

Counselors need the information that only parents can give them.
They can obtain it either in writing or through discussion. Because
the emphasis in this book is on the face-to-face interactions between
parents and counselors, written parental communications are considered only briefly here. Major consideration is given to the way
counselors can gather information in face-to-face encounters.

WRITTEN COMMUNICATIONS

A very useful way to tap parental knowledge is through parent-
completed case history questionnaires. As questionnaires are cur-
rently used, the parent is usually instructed to supply information
before an interview. The interview gives the parent an opportunity
to elaborate on, clarify, and update the information. It should be
noted that the questionnaire is often the first contact between a
counselor and a given parent.

Written parental messages also include anecdotal records kept
by parents. For example, parents sometimes are asked to write
descriptions of their children's behavior or of certain interactions
between themselves and their children, such as keeping records of

mealtime or bedtime behaviors or interactions. Notes, such as those parents write to teachers, are another means of written parental communication.

Some counselors use a questionnaire as a follow-up to discussion. For example, Falck (1976) reported a series of studies in which parents helped to design a questionnaire that was then sent to a larger number of parents. Falck discussed information obtained in these ways and the potential uses of the information.

These written forms constitute one way that parents can express themselves. Thus written parental communications are important. As Bissel (1976) pointed out, counselors should gratefully utilize items written by parents and should show them the same respect and consideration given to messages transmitted verbally.

LISTENING TO PARENTS' CONVERSATION

Perhaps the quickest way to gain parental information is through listening to their dialogue. A conversational situation enables parents to present information in depth, to elaborate on topics the counselor wants to know more about, and to discuss at length issues the parent or counselor feels are important. Thus the writer thinks that dialogue is the most efficient way to obtain the most, and the richest, information from parents.

The fact that one collects rich and varied information by actively listening to another is sometimes overlooked by counselors, particularly inexperienced ones. Counselors should be aware that much information is revealed by indirect means and in the context of conversation that seems to move from one topic to another, that is, in unstructured conversation. Perhaps this excerpt from an interview will illustrate the amount of information that can be obtained from a mother whose conversation seems to stray from the stated topic. The conversation took place at a first interview. The case history she supplied about her 4-year-old son, Darrell, indicated a rather stormy infancy.

> C: I notice you reported that Darrell was wakeful and restless as an infant; I'd like to know more about that period.

MRS. A: The biggest problem was that he almost never slept. I'd
lay him down in bed and he'd start crying. At first I let
him cry—the doctor told me to let him cry it out—but
he'd cry so hard his face would turn bluish, and he'd
sound like he was choking. So I'd pick him up and walk
with him. Sometimes he'd stop crying for a few minutes
while I carried him, but then he'd tune up again. Nothing
stopped his crying for very long—not feeding, not walk-
ing, nothing! I wasn't ready for a baby who cried all the
time! Doreen had me spoiled I guess. Oh, she wasn't
perfect, and I had the usual nervousness you have with a
first child; and she had crying spells and one time she had
colic for 3 days. But she also smiled at us a lot and cooed
and made baby noises and usually seemed happy. Maybe
Doreen was an advanced baby; she walked before she
was a year old. That was a mess! She got into *everything,*
but at least she was curious. And both my husband and I
loved it when she started saying words we could understand. Of course, Doreen is the apple of my husband's
eye. We weren't home from the hospital an hour before
he was carrying her around the house and bragging about
how pretty she was. He still brags about her and never
sounds cross when he talks with her. And she's so inde-
pendent—nothing seems to scare her. She'll go right up to
a strange child and ask to play with her—or she'll walk up
to a group of children and say she wants to do what
they're doing. She's so far ahead of Darrell—she was
when she was 4—maybe he feels he can't compete with
her.

In this example the mother was almost reminiscing aloud, and
in the process was supplying information directly about Doreen. She
also pointed out contrasts between Darrell and Doreen, with the
implication that the parents responded quite differently to each.
Such a conversation can supply the counselor with many leads.

Counselors who wish to develop greater skill in acquiring information through listening to parental conversation are encouraged to
experiment with various forms of the first practice exercise at the
end of this chapter, noting carefully the items of information they
obtain by this means.

MAKING LEADING STATEMENTS

Leading statements offer a second means by which counselors obtain information. To review, leading statements are those designed to elicit additional parental conversation. Following are examples of how such statements are used to educe information.

Tell me more about yourself.

I've wondered about how you manage to keep up with the activities of six children.

Let's talk about some ways that you have used to praise Mary for what she does well.

I'd like to hear your opinions about John's school program.

I'd like to know how Mary is doing now that she has her new braces.

Such statements give parents freedom to choose the words they want to use and freedom to respond with more than one or two words if they choose to do so. Counselors use leading statements as a way to convey the message, "I am not seeking a discrete, specific response, but I'd like to know more about this topic." Counselors' leading statements help parents to organize the information they wish to present because the topic for discussion is stated. Beyond stating the topic, the counselor does not limit what the parent can report.

Leading statements also can be used to clothe counselors' questions. Each of the statements in the example above can be converted into a question. Thus leading statements can be thought of as an indirect form of questioning. Leading statements have limited usefulness as indirect questions because they do not yield precise answers. For example, if the counselor wants to know, "How old were you when your child was born?" this information may not be revealed in response to the statement, "Tell me more about yourself." However if the counselor's question is, "What can you tell me about yourself?" then "Tell me more about yourself" is a useful substitute. When counselors want specific answers to specific questions, they should ask those questions directly. If counselors want rich and helpful details, leading statements can be substituted nicely for questions.

ASKING QUESTIONS

Although parental answers to questions are a rich source of information, there are a number of pitfalls that may be encountered in the use of questions. The first danger in questioning is that the counselor may set up a question–answer format for counseling sessions and allow sessions to deteriorate into what may be perceived as oral quizzes. The first reason to guard against such a quiz format is that it precludes other meaningful dialogue. One need only watch one or two TV quiz shows to realize how little one learns about the participants. Counselors want to understand both the information and the people who supply the information; that is, they want to do everything possible to increase, rather than decrease, their opportunities for understanding. Therefore counselors will shun a format that limits their knowledge and understanding of parents.

Benjamin (1974) cautioned against the overuse of questions. He contended that counselors who relied almost exclusively on the question–answer format were likely to be perceived as authorities who selected what was right or wrong to talk about or who knew all that was important to consider. Benjamin pointed out that a counselor who overused questions could be perceived as making judgments about the rightness or wrongness of parental answers to questions. If parents formed and maintained such impressions of a counselor, it would hinder both their desire and their ability to give information.

Having just considered reasons for not turning counseling sessions into question and answer periods, readers may wonder, "Should I *ever* ask a question?" Of course you should, and you can ask many appropriate ones. Counselors need only be careful (a) to clarify the attitudes from which their questions arise; (b) to intersperse questions with the other types of verbalizations that occur naturally in conversation; and (c) to use question forms that are likely to yield the type of information desired.

It is important that counselors consider their intentions in questioning parents. Counselors should not want to question parents in order to pin them down, to challenge, or to test them. Neither should counselors use questions to try to elevate themselves by showing how wise they are to conceive of such a profound question. Instead, counselors should ask questions in order to become better educated. With this motivation they will more likely experience the advantages and avoid the pitfalls of interjecting questions.

Question Forms

Counselor questions can be categorized according to their form, that is, either closed or open. Open questions have also been referred to as open-ended or leading questions (Richardson, Dohrenwend & Klein, 1965; Benjamin, 1974). Closed and open questions are asked for different reasons. Closed questions are designed to yield brief and specific answers. Open questions are designed to encourage the respondent to supply a greater number of details or to talk at greater length; in this respect open questions resemble leading statements.

The following are examples of closed questions: "How old is Johnny?" "Is he 5 or 6 years old?" "Do you live within the city limits?" "Do you spank Johnny?" Each of these questions can be answered with a word or two, or with a short phrase.

The following are open questions: "How is Johnny doing in reading?" "How do you feel?" "What does George do when he's angry?"

This writer has suggested subdividing the open category into *open-ended general questions* and *open-ended questions on a topic* (Webster, 1974). In open-ended general questions the topic is unspecified; for example, "How are you feeling?" "How's it going?" "What do you think?" These three general open-ended questions become open-ended questions on a topic when appropriately modified; for example, "How are you feeling about your mother-in-law's visit?" "How is your new job going?" "What do you think about George's reading?" The open-ended question on a topic differs from the general open-ended form only because a topic is specified within the question itself.

In several studies (Webster, 1974; 1976) parents were found to talk longer in response to counselor's open-ended questions than in response to closed questions. It was also found that open-ended questions on a topic led to the greatest amount of parental talking time. Because parental talking time is positively related to the amount of information parents provide, these findings suggest that counselors will learn more if they make liberal use of the open-ended question with the topic specified.

It should be noted that in the process of conversation it may be difficult to distinguish between general open-ended questions and open-ended questions on a topic. For example, a man told a counselor, "I just can't seem to get him [his son] interested in spending time with me. Whenever I suggest we do something together he either doesn't like the idea or says, 'I'm busy now, Dad,' or something like that.'' The counselor asked, ''And how do you feel then?'' The counselor's question might seem to be of the general form, but in context of the conversation it was clearly a question on the topic.

Question Content

Questions can also be classified generally according to their content. The following classification scheme for analysis of question content was suggested earlier (Webster 1974; 1976), and is useful in considering the content of parents' questions.

The first class of question content is *Request for Facts* (RF questions). These are questions that ask for information. Examples of RF questions include ''What is a sensorineural hearing loss?'' ''How long is this interview going to last?'' ''What is the fee for this service?'' and ''Is he supposed to wear his leg braces at night too?''

Cole (1975) and Marshall (1975) found that trained observers could identify RF questions with a high degree of consistency. Apparently the questioner's use of the word *what* served as a clue to listeners that an RF question was being asked.

In the second type of question, the *Request for Opinions* (RO question), the questioner directly or indirectly asks for another's opinion. Examples of RO questions are ''Do you think I should spank him when he acts that way?'' ''What should I do?'' and ''Do you feel this program will help her motor problems?'' A clue that one person is requesting another's opinion may be the use of ''Do you think'' or ''Do you feel.'' These words may be used in the question or they may be implied, as in ''What (in your opinion) should I do?''

The third content category is the *Request for Clarification* (RC questions). Here the questioner seems to desire elaboration of an idea or topic. Examples of RC questions include ''Do you mean ——?'' ''Are you saying——?'' and ''Do I understand you to say——?''

The final question category is the *Request for Discussion* (RD questions). Although RD questions may resemble RF or RO, the intent of the questioner seems to be to initiate discussion of a topic, rather than to ask for facts, opinions, or clarification. Examples of RD questions are ''Can we talk about discipline?'' ''All the new toys seem so complicated; what are you giving your children for Christmas?" and "Are any of you going to try acupuncture for your kids?"

Cole (1975) and Marshall (1975) found lower reliability among trained observers in classifying RC and RD questions than in classifying RF and RO questions. However Cole and Marshall found that interjudge agreement was high enough to justify including RC and RD categories in the question classification scheme.

Question Meaning

In addition to form and content, each question also has its meanings; in other words, there are attitudes, intentions, and ideas from which the question arises. Cole and Marshall in their unpublished papers (1975) showed that although trained observers could quite easily classify the form and content of parents' questions, the form and content did not reveal the meaning of any question. It was virtually impossible for observers to listen to a question and assess the reason that the question was asked; neither could they determine much about the internal state of the questioner by analyzing the form or content of the question. This finding is quite understandable because the meaning of a question is subject to at least two variables: the questioner's general life situation and particular internal state at the moment. Counselors should recognize that they cannot know the meaning of a question; they can only inquire further about its meaning, either through leading statements or direct questions.

Counselors use both closed and open questions in attempting to gain needed information from parents, and ask RF, RO, RC, and RD questions to elicit various types of information. Counselors should familiarize themselves with the process of judicious questioning and with the various types of questions.

Other Considerations in Questioning

As stated earlier, counselors should not use questions as an indirect means to challenge or confront parents. Benjamin (1974) believed that counselors may seem to challenge parents when they use questions that start with the word *why*. He contended that from childhood people learn to defend themselves when asked why. They feel they must explain or defend against such questions as, "Why did you spill that milk?" "Why did you hit your sister?" "Why are you late getting home?" or "Why did you do that?" According to Benjamin, the tendency to become defensive when confronted with *why* questions carries over into later life situations. For example, a parent may feel threatened in a situation in which a counselor asks "Why did you do that?" or "Why do you feel that way?" The counselor's intention may not be to challenge or dispute the parent; but nevertheless, the *why* question may be interpreted a challenge. If counselors follow this thinking and wish to avoid *why* questions, they can do so with relative ease. First, they can substitute *what* for *why* in their questions.

Counselors also can pay attention to their manner of speaking when they ask questions. A counselor's request for information can be delivered with such force, loudness, or rapidity that it invites threat or argument. Conversely, if the counselor's intent is to respect the parent, the loudness, force, and rate will be consistent with this attitude. Readers can illustrate this point for themselves by saying the following questions aloud several times, each time trying to convey a different attitude.

You didn't want to do that, did you?
What did you say?
You say he can't tell time?
Can't you tell him how you feel about that?

This exercise can underscore the fact that while the form and content of the question are important and should receive careful consideration, it is more important that counselors examine and clarify the attitudes from which their questions emerge. Questions for information should stem only from attitudes such as respectful curiosity or a desire to know and understand.

Another factor that should be mentioned when considering counselors' questions is the human tendency to ask several questions at once, or to ask questions within a question, thus producing run-on questions. An example of a run-on question is "What did you think about John's lying to you, or how did you feel, and have you decided what to do?" Such an outburst forces a parent to make a choice: Should she respond to the question about what was thought, or about what was felt, or about what action had been considered? Counselors who wish to gather as much information as possible in the shortest time will avoid asking several questions at once, because it requires that a parent choose which question to answer and thus slows parental response. This type of question is particularly troublesome when the counselor wishes to elicit a specific item of information, because the parent may choose to answer a part of the question that is unrelated to the information being sought.

Counselors also may have the human tendency to overexplain their questions. This can result in another form of run-on question, that is, a question that is asked several different ways. For example, a counselor asked a mother, "Who is Tim's doctor, you know, the doctor you saw recently, who prescribed the sedative you give Tim at night; what is his name, you know——?" One might guess the counselor in this example was so eager to have the question understood that she almost obscured it with added details. I have collected many examples of parental compassion for such counselor dilemmas, including the kind way the mother interrupted the above run-on question to say gently, "It's OK, dear, I know what you're trying to say. His name is Mason."

Counselors will sometimes catch themselves using run-ons because there are so many variables that prompt them to ververbalize a question. Counselors who use questions to obtain information will do well to practice asking questions that are simple, direct, and devoid of a long series of nonessential details. Specific suggestions for such practice are given in the study guides at the end of this chapter.

SUMMARY

Counselors gather much useful information in their face-to-face interactions with parents. Procedures for obtaining information include active listening as parents engage in dialogue, use of leading statements, and use of questions. Question forms and content deserve counselor attention, but counselors cannot judge a question's meaning by analyzing its form or content. It is suggested that counselors practice the judicious use of questions.

STUDY GUIDES FOR CHAPTER 8

Additional Readings

Benjamin, A. The helping interview (2nd ed.). Boston: Houghton-Mifflin, 1974, chap. 5.

Bissell, N. Communicating with parents of exceptional children. In E. Webster (Ed.), *Professional approaches with parents of handicapped children.* Springfield: Charles C. Thomas, 1976, chap. 8.

Garrett, A. *Interviewing: Its principles and methods.* New York: Family Service Association of America, 1942, Part I.

Richardson, S., Dohrenwend, B., & Klein, D. *Interviewing: Its forms and functions.* New York: Basic Books, 1965, pp. 142–150.

Webster E. Studies involving parents of children with communication handicaps. *Acta Symbolica,* 1974, *5:* 25–38.

Practice Exercises

1. Tape record several 5-minute conversations between you and one other person. During these 5 minutes your goal is to have the other person inform you. Analyze the tapes to determine each item of information you received and which of your behaviors seemed best to prompt the information from the other person. Consider what else you might have done to increase the likelihood of the person's sharing information. Give particular attention to the participants' relative amounts of talking time. Note carefully your communication patterns; did you sound interested, bored, challenging, enthusiastic, etc.? Also note your questions; practice re-asking questions that dissatisfied you.

2. Classify the following questions according to their form as closed (C), open-ended general (OEG), or open-ended on a topic (OET). You will find the writer's classification in Appendix B.

   a. What is the temperature in this room?
   b. Who did you see first, Bob or Bill?
   c. What can you tell us about the train wreck?
   d. What do you think you can do when George teases Mary?
   e. What are your reactions when George teases Mary?
   f. What happens when Jerry brings home poor spelling tests?
   g. What can you tell us?
   h. Are you sure that Jerry told you the truth?
   i. What makes you feel sure that Jerry told you the truth?

j. When Jerry told you about the incident, why were you sure he told you the truth?

k. What is his dog's name?

l. How are things going?

9

Giving Information

Counselors both need information from parents and are responsible for giving parents necessary and appropriate information. There seems to be an almost endless number and variety of situations in which information is conveyed to parents. Examples include a teacher conducting a parent conference to discuss a child's school progress; a pediatrician discussing his diagnosis of a child and his plans for treatment; a social worker visiting a home to help a family understand how to avail itself of treatment facilities; and a speech, hearing, or language clinician explaining a child's language status to his parents and informing them of therapy possibilities. In each of the examples, a counselor is conducting an informative session.

In exploring the process of information giving, counselors should remember that, although it is extremely necessary and useful to inform parents, informing is only one counselor function. The information function will be effective only if counselors serve the other functions concurrently. In other words, effective counselors should not let their parent conferences deteriorate into merely information giving sessions. Ways of guarding against such narrow use of counseling time are discussed in this chapter.

There are two avenues by which counselors give information. First, counselors plan activities designed to present knowledge and ideas they consider useful; for example, a teacher may plan a demonstration of a teaching strategy as a means of showing parents what she is doing in her classroom. Second, counselors present knowledge and ideas in response to parents' questions; the teacher in the previous example may ask for parental questions and share further information as a result of these questions. Each of these avenues for information giving is discussed in this chapter.

PLANNING INFORMATIVE SESSIONS

Information giving may be the easiest of the four counselor functions because each counselor has areas of expertise about which to inform others. It may also be true that it is easier to give information in counselor-planned sessions than in response to questions. Structuring a situation in advance may be easier than thinking on one's feet. Nevertheless, planning informative activities is a difficult task. A counselor needs not only to have accurate information and to report it accurately, but also must be aware of parental needs and limitations such as those discussed below.

Parents can absorb and use only a certain amount of information at any one time. They can feel bewildered when inundated with too much information all at once. For example, McDonald (1962) cites the case of the mother of a cerebral palsied child who insisted that a counselor give her detailed information about her child's treatment plan. The counselor outlined the beginning treatment plan. When the mother asked for further information, the counselor demurred. When the mother continued to press the issue, asking repeatedly about further plans, the counselor tried to detail the entire 6-year program she envisioned for the child. The mother, recognizing that she was unable to understand and cope with this enormously complex and detailed information, asked the counselor to stop. Later the mother recognized that perhaps she was asking questions that couldn't yet be answered. Perhaps the counselor could have helped the mother to clarify her need for so much information at one time if she had recognized that sometimes parents ask for more information than they can assimilate. It is difficult for counselors to pace themselves, especially in the face of parental pressure, so that parents receive appropriate amounts of information but not so much as to be confusing or overwhelming.

Parents need different types of information at different times, and counselors are called on to supply not only the amount but also the type of information that is needed. For example, it is obviously inappropriate to present suggestions about toilet training to parents whose children have long since passed that stage, and no counselor who is sensitive to parents would to so. However there are many more subtle choices to be made in selecting the type of information to present.

In deciding on the appropriateness of any item of information to be presented, the sensitive counselor will first listen to what the parent says about himself, his child, and his general life situation. Counselors should remember that parents will reveal those areas in which they need information through their statements or questions. The counselor's role is to listen and to note the areas that seem to interest the parent or in which there is parental confusion. Perhaps the counselor will have to ask questions to determine how much information the parent already has. In short, counselors can plan their information giving from a parent-supplied baseline.

Having assessed the parent's need for information, counselors will find many aids to planning informative activities. Counselors can tap not only their own training and experience but also numerous materials prepared for informing parents or families. It is appropriate to use various audiovisual materials such as those contained in instructional media centers in schools or in university and college libraries, to schedule guest speakers, to plan panel discussions, and so forth. An excellent resource for parents is Weiner's *Help for the Handicapped Child* (1973). This book can also serve as a resource for counselors as they plan discussion topics or information giving activities. The journal *Exceptional Parent* is also an excellent source of ideas.

Many counselors who see parents regularly, and who can determine that they have a reading level that is adequate for the task, like to use what has been termed *bibliotherapy*. This involves reading and discussing of articles, chapters, or entire books. Doernberg, Bernard, and Lenz (1976) pointed out that reading material can be used to generate parents' ideas about their behaviors and to stimulate discussion among parents meeting in groups. However, Mc-Williams (1976) described three pitfalls that counselors should be aware of if they wish to use bibliotherapy: (a) authors often disagree on their explanations of phenomena and such differences of opinion can be confusing to some parents; (b) authors may oversimplify their explanations and some parents will resent the simplistic solutions to what they know to be enormously complex problems; and (c) authors may use terms that confuse parents. To these cautions, another can be added: Some parents can view reading as a complicated and unwanted extra burden; in such cases the counselor may want to do the homework and discuss the ideas contained in the reading.

In all information giving sessions, parents need to discuss the material presented if they are to understand and use it. The question of how to provide for parental discussion within an informative activity can challenge counselors.

A counselor can provide adequate time for discussion by dividing one topic into several subtopics. Such segmenting is highly desirable. For example, the topic of the development of motor skills by the child with cerebral palsy can be divided into numerous subtopics. Further, if the counselor does not plan to discuss segments of so broad a topic, parents probably will do so in order to be able to deal with it.

Another counselor option is to plan discussion of one broad topic over several sessions. For example, in a program conducted and reported by Wyatt (1969), mothers spent several sessions discussing "corrective feedback" and the benefits of such feedback as part of the process of reading to their children. Mothers then practiced this procedure in additional sessions.

A counselor-planned informative activity will probably never match perfectly with all the needs of a parent or group of parents. Fortunately, perfection is not the goal; perserverance in attempting to meet parents' needs for information is the goal. Informative activities will be less subject to error as counselors listen to the needs expressed by each parent and plan activities that speak to these expressed needs.

GIVING INFORMATION IN RESPONSE TO
PARENTS' QUESTIONS

In the last chapter it was stated that counselors use questions that can be classified as closed, open-ended general, and open-ended on a topic. Parents use these same question forms. It was also pointed out that counselors ask questions that can be further categorized as RF (requests for facts), RO (requests for opinions), RC (requests for clarification), and RD (requests for discussion). Parents also ask all of these types of questions.

Parents' RF Questions

Parental RF questions are a primary means of assisting counselors to give information. Parents' RF questions may differ from those asked by counselors; for example, parents may ask such questions as, "What is a learning disability?" "Is he reading on a second-grade level?" "Will the bus pick him up each day?" and "What does *reinforcement* mean?"

The counselor's first responsibility in dealing with a parent's RF question is to provide the information requested. Often the counselor may wonder why the parent asked the question; if so, the counselor should first give the information, then inquire about what prompted the question. This order is desirable because of the counselor's responsibility to provide parents with facts.

Once the counselor has relayed the information requested, discussion is possible. Counselors should remember that discussion of a topic can be extremely limited when only one participant is knowledgeable about it. Consider the absurdity of the following discussion between a counselor and the mother of a girl with a repaired cleft palate.

M: The doctor doesn't want to take out her tonsils for fear her voice would get worse. How could that happen?

C: You'd hate for her voice to get worse, wouldn't you? And you're afraid that might happen.

M: Yes, but what do her tonsils have to do with her voice?

C: They may have a lot to do with amount of nasality she exhibits, although that seems strange to you. Are you concerned about it?

In this example the counselor behaved as if the mother had the facts, or did not need them, although the mother began by revealing that she did not understand the physician's reasoning. The woman was helpless to do more than re-ask her question; the counselor's refusal to answer the question precluded any discussion of the topic.

Certainly no sensitive counselor would want to be caught in

such a scene, but probably most of us have at one time or another openly or subtly asked parents to discuss information that they had not yet acquired. It seems more sensible, and places much less burden on parents, to give them the information they request and to follow the explanation with an opportunity for discussion.

When a parent asks a question, the counselor may need time to formulate a response, and the need for thinking time is nothing for which to be apologetic. Counselors should not use the smoke screen of meaningless (or potentially detrimental) verbalization in an attempt to hide the fact that parental questions are worthy of carefully formulated answers.

When counselors have their information at hand, they should give definite answers. They will sound vague or unsure if they make statements such as "a cleft palate seems to be . . ." rather than "a cleft palate is defined as . . ." Counselors who overqualify statements of fact can sound ill-trained or ill-prepared, although in fact they may be trying to be overly cautious in their use of language.

On the other hand, no person can know all the answers to all the questions that parents generate. When counselors do not have the information requested, they should say so. If a counselor is unsure of the facts, the most sensible response is, "I'm not sure, but I'll find out and let you know." The counselor can then proceed to learn the facts. Parents will not tolerate an "I don't know" every time a question is asked, but they respect persons who can delay answering until able to give an accurate report.

If these factors are kept in mind, RF items are usually not troublesome. The following examples of parental questions are offered to illustrate how much information counselors might provide in response to RF items.

Do 3-year-olds usually play together for more than a few minutes at a time?

We're moving to Houston. How can I find out about special education classes for him there?

I understand there is an operation to cure nerve deafness. Is this true?

I don't understand how an auditory perception problem can affect reading. How can this happen?

Why does this school limit its classes to 12 kids?

There is one aspect of parents' RF questions that is sometimes troublesome to beginning counselors. Sometimes these counselors say they are afraid to give parents factual information, fearing that if parents knew facts they would be more anxious rather than less so. Such fear of parental reaction can block a counselor's spontaneous responses; it can prompt the counselor to withhold certain types of information, to dilute or sugarcoat negative facts, and to overlook or obscure some facts that might be useful to parents.

Many counselors, including this one, can recall situations in which they were tempted to distort or withhold information on the assumption that parents must be protected. Parents do not need this kind of protection; to engage in it hinders parents from facing and dealing with their realities instead of helping them. Counselors probably hesitate to share certain information with certain parents for a number of reasons.

One major reason is that counselors have confused description and evaluation, a very human tendency. Counselors should remember that information giving is an exercise in description. Evaluation has no place in the process until after the facts are presented. Evaluation is likely to stir parental anxiety and defensiveness. Description is less likely to stir negative emotions.

The second reason a counselor may hesitate to give a parent information is a matter of projection. The counselor may think that if he were in the parent's place, he would consider certain information to have negative connotations and would then be upset. For example, the counselor might think, "If I were that parent, I'd be hurt and anxious if I knew my child had cerebral palsy." The counselor who thus projected his own world onto the parent might hesitate to say the child has cerebral palsy. Although counselors should be aware that knowing the facts about a child can constitute a crisis for a parent, not knowing the facts is even more threatening. Most parents want to know the facts, want help to cope with the facts, and do not want information cluttered by counselor evaluation. Generally, parents can be trusted to cope with their life situations better if they have current information and can understand how this information was gathered.

Counselors can choose the types of language they use. They can be careful to describe and to delay judgment. They will find that the exercise of such caution also helps them to clarify their projections.

Parents' RO Questions

When parents request opinions (ask RO questions), they may be asking for facts; or they may think they are doing so. Counselors may have to remind themselves that statements of opinion are not the same as statements that describe data. Opinions are either inferences or evaluations. Parents are entitled to know counselors' opinions, but opinions should be given cautiously.

Some counselors seem extremely reluctant to give opinions; some believe that if they do so parents may view them as dogmatic or "preachy." That reasoning seems unfortunate because when anyone holds dogmatic attitudes, they will be revealed in various ways, not just in statements of opinion. In other words, counselors will give nonverbal clues to what their opinions are, even if they don't state them directly. Here again, counselors' attitudes are the important variables. If counselors respect parents and thus exercise rational authority, their opinions will be voiced simply as opinions and not as pronouncements. These counselors will not sound as if they openly or subtly insist that their opinions be accepted.

Many authors, among them Stewart (1974) and Murphy (1976), believe that counselors have a responsibility to state their opinions, and it is imperative that they make such statements when parents ask them to do so. It seems that counselors who interact most successfully with parents are the ones who are generous—generous with their ideas and their opinions, and generous in granting parents the right to reject their opinions.

OTHER CONSIDERATIONS IN INFORMATION GIVING

The foregoing statements about information giving should not be construed to suggest that if counselors do their best to impart information, parents will immediately understand and accept those facts presented. This is simply not the case. Parents arrive at understanding at their own pace for various reasons outside the counselor's control. As has been pointed out previously, one deterrent to parental understanding is the interference created by internal reactions. When such reactions arise, even the parent who has requested factual information may be unable to assimilate it. Counselors should be aware of this phenomenon and should recognize that parents may need time to discuss their internal reactions before they can adjust to the information. With such additional time and help, most parents seem to be able to understand and act appropriately when they are given information.

Avoiding Jargon

Professionals are often tempted to try to talk about people or events in jargon, that is, in terms that either refer to broad category labels or are unique to certain professions. Some professionals seem to use such jargon in an effort to impress, but more often they seem unaware that elaborate terminology can obscure rather than promote understanding. The following two examples are illustrative.

A speech clinician explained carefully to a mother, "Your little girl had a Type IV cleft. Even with surgery she has considerable velopharyngeal incompetence, and I'd like to refer her to a surgeon to see if he thinks a pharyngeal flap procedure would be desirable or whether he'd suggest exploring the prosthetics route.

Such language might give information to professionals like plastic surgeons, otolaryngologists, or speech clinicians, but it is probably nothing more than noise to the mother.

A teacher reported to the parents of an 8-year-old child in her special class, "James seems to have an auditory perception problem that affects his reading. I thought he might also have a visual perceptual problem, but he performed so well on the Frostig that I don't really think visual processing is involved. We will test further with the ITPA and then perhaps start James on an i/t/a program."

Any parent who is not also professionally trained may be lost in the maze of professional jargon. Even those who are professionally trained may have great difficulty sorting this verbiage.

In response to such jargon, other professionals may nod wisely and act as if they know exactly what is being said. In fact they often are at as much loss as parents to know the specific facts to which the terms refer. Jargon does not describe the behavior or status of a person and thus can easily be misunderstood.

Use of jargon is not exclusively a problem of professional persons. Parents have been heard to use jargon, for example, to refer to their children as "uncooperative," "easily frustrated," "withdrawn," "stubborn," "lazy," and so forth. These terms are not descriptive; they tell more about the parents' reactions than about their children's behaviors.

The value of skill in description cannot be overemphasized. Counselors can practice understanding. As they practice, counselors will quickly see the value of examples as an aid to explanation.

It is also useful to describe things fairly slowly, interspersing examples. Such a pace gives listeners a chance to perceive and absorb messages. Many people tend to speak quite rapidly, especially when they are very familiar with a topic. From the point of view of the listening parent, it is particularly difficult to absorb new ideas when they come thick and fast. If counselors will tape-record several conversations, they can assess their amount and rate of speaking, their use of simple terms, and their use of examples to explain.

Assessing Parental Understanding

However specifically conveyed, information is not useful unless it is clearly perceived and understood. Therefore it is important that counselors try to insure that parents receive and understand information as it was intended. To this end, various probes can be used.

It seems unwise to probe with such global questions as, "Do you understand?" "Do you see what I mean?" or "Do you follow me?" The primary reason for avoiding such nonspecific questions is that many persons will answer in the affirmative, whether or not they really do understand. A second reason for discarding nonspecific probes is that they reveal nothing about the extent of a person's understanding.

A counselor will get a more accurate picture of a parent's perception of information, and of the parent's ability to use it, if more specific probes are used. More useful means of assessing understanding are suggested in the following examples.

A clinician explained to the mother of a 4-year-old boy the

recommendation that he have speech therapy and outlined her plan for providing this therapy. Upon finishing her explanation, the counselor said to the mother, "I know you'll have to explain this plan to your husband so that he'll understand it too. What do you think he'll consider most important?"

A social worker informed the mother of a 6-year-old boy that the school recommended the child be given a psychological evaluation. The worker detailed reasons and specified plans for carrying out this testing. She then said to the mother, "I want to be sure my explanation has been clear. Would you please tell me how you understand what I've said so that I can try to clear up any part where I may have confused you."

A group of parents of hearing-impaired 2-year-olds had watched a film about young deaf children. At the film's conclusion the counselor said, "There are a lot of ideas contained in the film. Let's organize our discussion around the ideas that you think you can use at home. Mrs. Jones, why don't you start?"

In all of these examples the counselor's intent was to help people state in their own words what they understood or considered useful. If counselors wish to make an adequate assessment of parental understanding, they will not ask parents to parrot professional jargon, but will ask them to explain the information in ther own words. If a parent can do so, understanding probably is adequate. Parents also reveal their understanding of information when they state how they will use it.

Such parental verbalizations are also helpful to the counselor who wishes to evaluate the usefulness or helpfulness of the information he chose to present. This is one of the many ways that parents help counselors to continue to learn.

SUMMARY

Information giving is both a relatively easy task and a very difficult one. Counselors can plan informative sessions or can give information in response to various types of parental questions. It is useful to employ simple descriptive language. Various probes for parental understanding are also useful.

Information giving can be helpful and stimulating to both parents and counselors. Counselors who wish to continue learning probably will find that trying to explain information prompts them to continue to acquire knowledge and to state it succinctly.

STUDY GUIDES FOR CHAPTER 9

Additional Readings

Bissell, N. Communicating with parents of excetional children. In E. Webster (Ed.) *Professional approaches with parents of handicapped children*. Springfield: Charles C. Thomas, 1976, Chap. 8.

Doernberg, N., Bernard, M., & Lenz, C. Psychoeducational treatment for parents of autistic children. In E. Webster (Ed.), *Professional approaches with parents of handicapped children*. Springfield: Charles C. Thomas, 1976, pp. 83–90.

McWilliams, B. Various aspects of parent counseling. In E. Webster (Ed.), *Professional approaches with parents of handicapped children*. Springfield: Charles C. Thomas, 1976, pp. 43–62.

Todd, M. & Gottlieb, M. Interdisciplinary counseling in a medical setting. In E. Webster (Ed.), *Professional approaches with parents of handicapped children*. Springfield: Charles C. Thomas, 1976, chap. 7.

Wyatt, G. *Language learning and communication disorders in children*. New York, The Free Press, 1969, chaps. 1 and 6.

Practice Exercises

1. List five professional or technical terms. They can be terms you have used or ones you have heard used by other persons. Look up the dictionary definition of any term about which you are unclear. Your task in this exercise is to explain each of these terms so that they can be understood by a nonprofessionally trained person. You may find it helpful to imagine that you are speaking to a person in high school or to one in a beginning college class.

2. Roleplay a situation in which you are the counselor working with a group of four parents. You can delineate the parents' roles as you wish. Your task is to plan a 15-minute information giving session for this group. Make explicit the bases on which you selected the information to

be presented. Show how you check on the parents' understanding and on the usefulness of this information to them. This activity can be repeated in various forms until you are more comfortable both with the process of explaining and with probing for understanding.

10

Helping Parents with Clarification

In context of sharing ideas and information, counselors help parents to clarify their thoughts, emotions, and attitudes. Clarification is the process of making aspects of one's world "more clear or easier to understand" (*American Heritage Dictionary of the English Language*, 1969, p. 247). Through discussion, roleplaying, and other procedures used in counseling sessions, parents are given opportunities to understand pertinent information. They are also given avenues for expressing and thus clarifying their attitudes and emotions.

It seems generally true that parents can be trusted to live increasingly creative and productive lives, including caring adequately for their children, provided that they can clearly see and move through some of the barriers that prevent their adequate functioning. That is, parents can manage their lives better as they can see more clearly what direction to take, and as they can perceive and work through some of the issues that may prevent their satisfaction and /or constructive behavior. One of the counselor's major functions is to help them perceive more clearly and deal more constructively with various issues.

THE IMPORTANCE OF CLARIFICATION

Clarification precedes action. Often this sequence is not recognized because the act of clarifying is so easily done. The need for clarification before one can act is more readily seen at times when it is a more difficult task. For example, when one who reads only English begins to cook a stew, understanding is fairly simple if the person has a recipe written in English. A clear grasp of the recipe is more difficult if the only available cookbook is written in French. In either case, understanding how to do it is the first step in preparing an acceptable stew.

The need for clarification also is obvious when one sets out to change a previously learned behavior. It is necessary to clearly perceive and describe what one is doing now before one can do something else instead. To use an example that applies to parent counseling, suppose that a counselor wishes to learn to speak more slowly and to interject pauses so that others may have a chance to speak. The task requires clarification of several aspects of current behavior before a permanent change can take place. The counselor must know the present speech rate and the frequency and duration of pauses: There must be a baseline against which to measure change. A beginning tape recording can be made to assist in establishing the baseline, and subsequent recordings can be compared with it. The counselor may also find it useful to clarify some of the reasons for wanting to use a slower rate of speech. The point is that one must clarify one's current status in order to know how one is different at a later time.

COUNSELOR ATTITUDES ABOUT CLARIFICATION

The importance and utility of clarification make it essential that counselors utilize several means to help parents engage in this process. There is no one simple way to help parents in this endeavor, but certain counselor attitudes seem to pay off better than others.

First, counselors must feel that clarification is important and that they can assist parents with this process. They will not serve this function well if they hold the attitude expressed by one counselor who said, "I give parents all the information I have. It's somebody else's job to help them understand it."

It is also important that counselors understand and accept the

fact that parents will try to clarify those issues *they* think are important, whether or not counselors think the issues deserve priority.
Conversely, counselors can tell parents they should understand certain issues, and parents may verbally agree, but they will not seek to
clarify any item unless they believe it really matters in their lives.

Finally, counselors must understand that they are not the only
resource for parents in the clarification process. When clarification
is a relatively simple task, a person usually can do it alone. It is
when clarification involves more complex issues or behaviors that
the person may arrive at understanding only by receiving outside
help. The need for outside help is exemplified by the reader of
English confronting a French cookbook; to understand it, he must
recruit the aid of someone who reads French. But counselors should
remember that parents arrive at many understandings without the
counselor's assistance. They sort out many issues on their own or in
discussions with other family members. Counselors should serve to
help parents understand and cope with those issues that elude perception or comprehension unless there is help from outside the
family.

Counselors will find that all of their interactions with parents
can be used for the purpose of clarification, in addition to any other
purpose the situation may serve. This function is continuous and it
is concurrent with every other function. Certainly clarification proceeds as parents give information. The acts of specifying and elabo-
rating important details require increasing clarity of perception. As
counselors give information to parents, they help them understand
how certain factors relate to the whole picture. Parents can be
helped to change behavior when such details are more clearly perceived and better understood.

Parents also serve as resources for each other in the clarification process. In multiperson groups parents can receive new ideas
and suggestions from other parents. These groups can also provide
opportunities for ventilation and clarification of emotions.

LISTENING AS MUTUAL CLARIFICATION

The ability to listen to understand is the single most important
asset of the person who wants to help parents clarify important
matters. Parents discuss more topics when interacting with an un-

derstanding listener; they also discuss subjects in greater depth. Parents must feel that the counselor is trustworthy before they will explore issues that, for whatever reason, they have failed to clarify previously. They must also feel that they have the counselor's respect. As a counselor attempts to follow a parent's thinking, to catch glimpses of how the parent feels, or to understand better the meaning a parent expresses, the counselor evidences a desire to behave respectfully and in trustworthy fashion. As stated earlier (Webster, 1972), counselors who can delay judgment and listen to understand will help to create an atmosphere that is free of threat, in which a parent may seize the opportunity to explore and clarify issues.

Actually, because active listening requires the listener to formulate and express hunches, clarification becomes a reciprocal process. It is a two-way street traveled by both speaker and listener. The counselor tries to follow the parent's lead and seeks to clarify his impressions about the meanings expressed. The counselor makes such statements as, "Tell me more about that, I don't quite understand," or "I hear you saying that . . ." or the counselor asks such questions as, "Does it seem to you that . . . ?" "Do you mean that . . . ?" "How is that related to . . . ?" As the counselor searches for greater understanding, such statements or questions also give the parent opportunities for clarification. The parent can rethink the intended meaning, and can sort and refine it so that it may be expressed more fully, clearly, and accurately.

Clarification, then, becomes mutual when active listening takes place. This type of counselor listening provides opportunities for each participant to make issues or ideas clearer and easier to understand.

Again, it is relatively unimportant whether the counselor's hunches are right or wrong. An erroneous guess, made in the spirit of trying to understand, provides the parent with a good opportunity to look more closely at the verbalization, to analyze the more correct meaning, and to think how it might be stated. The following example will illustrate this point.

The mother of a 12-year-old boy with an orthopedic disability, who had only recently begun to walk without crutches, met with a counselor in a two-person session. They discussed the boy's delight on the previous evening when he walked from his bedroom to the kitchen.

Mrs. O: He was so proud! It *is* really something else to watch him . . . the first time I got big tears in my eyes. I thought this day would never come! I also thought, "Oh Lord, he's so proud and it's really only a drop in the bucket . . . he has so far to go and he's so far behind . . . he goes so slow, so slow."

C: You mean you can't really feel pleased because you know what problems he still has?

Mrs. O: Oh no, I don't mean I'm not pleased! Oh no, I'm thrilled! I just can't help thinking . . . You know, maybe that's one of my problems. I get to thinking and I can't let him know how thrilled I am . . . like last night.

C: You couldn't show your excitement?

Mrs. O: I guess not . . . no, I know I didn't . . . so busy thinking discouraged . . . I wonder why. . . .

Their conversation continued. Perhaps Mrs. O, through trying to correct the counselor's impression, began to gain some insight into impressions she conveyed elsewhere.

Clarification of any issue cannot take place all at once. Neither can it be hurried. Furthermore, counselors cannot force or cajole parents into engaging in the process of clarification. But as they listen and try to understand parental meanings, counselors often recognize that clarification is taking place. Or parents report later that a counseling session helped them figure out something of importance. Such a statement is tantamount to reporting that clarification took place, or began, during the session.

SUGGESTING FACTORS TO BE CLARIFIED

Parents can profit by clarifying any or all of the factors discussed in Chapter 4. Parents often need assistance to understand and cope with their concerns. They may need to perceive more clearly those factors influencing their aspirations for themselves and/or their children, and to adjust their standards when they are unrealistic. Guilt is such a common emotion that most parents probably need clarification of issues and factors surrounding feelings of guilt. Certainly parents need to perceive, explore, and develop such emotions as joy, pleasure, and satisfaction.

There is, of course, no clear demarcation between those issues that are more worthy of clarification and those that are less worthy. A sensible rule of thumb is that if a parent thinks a certain issue or idea needs to be better understood, it is worthy of attention.

It is also helpful to remember that a person who begins to clarify one issue or idea is likely to discover additional issues or ideas that need to be worked on. The previous example of the mother of the orthopedically disabled boy illustrates this point. As she began to discuss her pleasure, she discovered another area in need of exploration. It could as easily have happened the other way around. She might have begun to discuss her worry about the future, or her discouragement with the boy's slow progress, and become increasingly aware of her feelings of pride and excitement. Thoughts, feelings, and attitudes are seldom single units. They tend to come in clusters. The process of discussing one part of the package stirs consciousness of numerous other parts. It is true, then, that parents suggest many of the factors they need to clarify.

However parents cannot possibly be aware of all the issues they need to understand, and the counselor must suggest some of them. When the counselor thinks a particular factor should be discussed, the parent should be informed of the counselor's impression. The counselor should also state the impression directly. Such confrontation need not be harshly or angrily done. When done in the spirit of respectful inquiry, confrontation is not demeaning to a parent. The following example illustrates one approach to direct confrontation.

George's parents arrived for a session talking angrily about George's school. On the previous day they had been informed of the teacher's recommendation that George be retained in the second grade because he was having extreme difficulty with reading. George's father was furious. He spoke twice about suing the teacher. The second time he threatened a lawsuit, his wife burst into tears. The counselor interrupted him to say, "Wait a minute, Mr. A. Before you decide to sue, there are some things to be understood here. What does this mean to you that makes you so angry?" Both parents talked somewhat more calmly about such factors as their high hopes for the boy, their fear that he would be labeled as a slow learner, and their inability to know how best to help him. Exploration of these issues occupied two counseling sessions. As he left the first one, Mr. A volunteered, "OK, I won't see my lawyer today, but I'm still mad!" The counselor responded gently, "Of course you are, and hurt, too." By the end of the second session, George's parents of course had not resolved all of their concerns about the boy, but Mr. A saw clearly that threatening a lawsuit did not solve any problems and could possibly create several others.

Usually the need for sorting out one's feelings is not as dramatic as the one exemplified above. Nevertheless, every time the counselor feels clarification is necessary, he should say so.

Counselors can suggest factors to be clarified with other statements and questions such as, "I think that's an important idea; can we pursue it further?" or "That seems to be an idea we need to talk more about," or "I'm interested in that point you just raised; can you tell more about it?" Counselors can also introduce suggestions with a sentence such as, "I'd like us to talk about [the subject] so that I can try to help you understand more about it." Roleplaying that proceeds from discussion often is helpful in the clarification process.

SUMMARY

Clarification is necessary before action can be taken and before behavior can be changed. Counselors serve this function as they give and receive information and as they help parents learn new behaviors. In addition, entire sessions can be devoted to helping parents clarify matters of importance to them. Some of the factors that need to be better understood are suggested by parents, and others are introduced by counselors.

STUDY GUIDES FOR CHAPTER 10

Additional Readings

Buscaglia, L. *The disabled and their parents: A counseling challenge.* Thorofare, New Jersey: Charles B. Slack, 1975, chap. 5.

Heisler, V. *A handicapped child in the family: A guide for parents.* New York: Grune & Stratton, 1972, chaps. 1, 5, 6, 10.

Wing, L. *Autistic children: A guide for parents and professionals.* New York: Brunner/Mazel, 1972, chap. 10.

Practice Exercises

1. Reread a number of the examples of counselor–parent interaction other than those in this chapter. Note those counselor statements or questions that could assist parents to understand their ideas, attitudes, or emotions.

2. Refer to the example of George's parents in this chapter. Speculate about what this mother could have felt as she began to cry. Speculate further about how you might help this mother see such factors more clearly.

3. Set up a 3- to 5-minute two-person conversation in which your goal is to help the person clarify ideas being expressed. You need not know the topic of conversation in advance. Your task is to delay judgment, to refrain from giving advice or making suggestions until you feel very sure that the person wants you to do so. After the conversation assess the ways in which you have functioned to promote the person's understanding. Note also the ways in which your ideas may have become more clear.

11

Helping Parents Change
Their Behaviors

The fourth counselor function is helping parents to learn new behaviors, which is also called parent education or training. Training is listed as the last of the counselor functions, not because it is least important, but because it requires the counselor to exercise all the other functions as training takes place. In other words, training is not a counselor–parent activity that should be separated from counseling. It should be considered to be a part of counseling. To be successful parent trainers, counselors must be skilled givers and receivers of information and must be able to help parents perceive and understand issues and ideas. When each of the other counselor functions operates in conjunction with training, parents have been shown to be able to learn an amazing number of behaviors.

HOW TRAINING UTILIZES COUNSELOR SKILLS

Thoughtful counselors will not decide that a certain behavior should be learned by all parents and then set out to teach it to all of those seen. Such predetermination may invite parental resistance and failure. Instead, counselors can listen and receive information about present parental behaviors, and about which of these seem to contribute to their problems. Parents can be counted on to discuss their own behavior in the context of discussing situations and events involving their children. They will also reveal problem areas. Counselors can ask parents to consider which of their behaviors they desire to change. Parental information can establish training priorities and suggest parental interest. To put all of this another way, parents can help to select and plan their own training activities. Such parental involvement will not automatically guarantee sustained parental motivation or ease of learning. There may be unclarified blind spots to prevent success. But when the parents themselves consider it worthwhile to learn a task, they are more likely to master it than when counselors dictate their learning.

This is not to say that parents have the sole right to suggest which of their behaviors may be important to change. Counselors share in choosing those parental behaviors that should be changed. This is another way counselors evidence rational authority and peership with parents. The counselor's ability to give information enters the picture here. When the counselor's experience indicates that a certain behavior is contributing to the parent's problem, the counselor should state that idea directly. The counselor must explain why the old behavior may not bring the desired results, what the parent might do instead, and how the parent can proceed to change.

Explaining the task (the target behavior) to be learned, and its potential benefits, is usually the first crucial step in parent training. Unless parents know what they are being asked to do, they will become confused. Unless they understand why the behavioral change may be important, they may view the task as trivial. The counselor who does not anticipate the need for explanation may be appalled the first time parents make statements such as, "I guess I know what I'm supposed to do, but I'm not sure," or "I know what you want me to do, but I don't for the life of me see why I'm learning to do this."

No matter whether the task to be learned is suggested first by parent or counselor, training inevitably will involve discussion. Parents will need opportunities to ask questions in order to understand the item to be trained and the counselor's rationale for it. They may need to clarify their thinking either before training or during it. As training progresses, parents may need to discuss and clarify their attitudes or emotions so that these do not interfere with their ability to learn.

Often training involves roleplaying. Some behaviors can more easily be demonstrated than described in words. Parental learning involves practice of new behavior, which can be accomplished through roleplaying during counseling sessions. For example, a mother thought she should learn to state her rules for her daughter simply and then refrain from arguing with the girl about them. She roleplayed setting limits with a second woman playing the child. The two women enacted a situation in which the mother explained briefly to the child that she could not go out with her friends after dark. The roleplayed child complained loudly and bitterly in an attempt to cajole the mother into changing the limit. The mother practiced several of the means by which she could disengage herself from continuing the argument with the girl.

Roleplaying has certain advantages as a parent training tool. It provides opportunities for parents to practice various options while free of the constraints of interacting with their own children. This freedom can be beneficial in the early stages of training. Through roleplaying, parents can try out various ways of behaving in order to choose the option that seems most comfortable and workable. The procedure also includes time for parents to discuss their thoughts about the behaviors they learn. Although roleplaying is not a substitute for the practice of a target behavior with those persons directly involved, it is useful in the preliminary stages of training.

Counselors may also find it useful to have parents observe another person demonstrating skills that parents will learn. This is the case, for example, when a counselor and mother watch a teacher or clinician model a specific procedure with a child. Here, again, information-giving skill is used as the counselor points out details of the behavior being demonstrated so that the parent can note them.

EXAMPLES OF PARENT TRAINING

The primary focus in parent training programs has been to teach parents how to teach or train their children. Some of the suggestions given to parents whose children are developing normally, such as those put forth by Ginott (1965), Gordon (1970), and Madsden and Madsden (1972), are also applicable to parents whose children exhibit various problems. Other programs are designed to teach special skills to parents of children with a particular type of disability, such as those discussed by Doernberg, Rosen, and Walker (1968), Horton (1968), Carrier (1970), Fraiberg (1969), Slater (1971), Badger (1972), Carpenter & Augustine (1973), and Simmons-Martin (1976).

There are training programs designed to help parents cope with their children's behavioral, emotional, or communication problems. Several examples of programs designed to help parents cope with such problem behaviors will be discussed briefly.

Gordon (1970) discussed the role of parental "put-down" messages in parent–child conflicts. He suggested several ways that parental speech to children could be changed so that neither would lose in any conflict between them.

Madsden and Madsden (1972) suggested techniques that parents could use to modify behaviors such as a child's complaining, amount of food intake, and lying. Veenstra (1971) and Badger (1972) reported programs that enabled mothers to modify a number of their children's negative behaviors. Behavior modification programs for parents were discussed by several authors in two comprehensive volumes (Mash, Hamerlynck, & Handy, 1976; Mash, Handy, & Hamerlynck, 1976).

Johnson and Katz (1973) summarized a number of studies using behavior modification techniques with children with severe emotional disturbances. Some of these studies suggested techniques parents could use at home. In his review of the literature on parent counseling, Leigh (1975) discussed several types of parent training programs. Wing's (1972) suggestions were written for parents and professionals who deal with autistic children. Also for professionals are training manuals for conducting behavior modification parent groups by Wikler, Savino, and Kyle (1976) and by Johnson, Devitt, and Bueno (1974).

In a slightly different vein, Wyatt (1969) trained mothers of young children with language or speech impairments. She observed that many mothers used elaborate language with their children. In the belief that simplified language provided a model children could imitate, she taught mothers to read and speak to their children in specified ways. Mothers' success was measured by improvement in children's language performance. Many of the children whose mothers read to them daily in the prescribed manner showed dramatic improvement in the language items that were measured.

The training of mothers to assist in their children's language development has been reported by other authors such as Bush and Bonachea (1973), Goldstein and Lanyon (1971), and Fudala (1973). Mothers have also been shown to be capable of modifying their children's articulatory behavior. Studies have been reported by Sommers (1962), Sommers, Furlong, Rhodes, Fichter, Bowser, Copetas, and Saunders (1964), and Sommers, Shilling, Paul, Copetas, Bowser, and McClintock (1959).

Parents are not the only family members who have been trained to modify children's behavior. For example, Wyatt (1976) reported on a summer camp program in which siblings were trained in various behavior modification procedures to use with their retarded brothers and sisters. When they saw the constructive ways the retarded children performed for the siblings, many parents learned the behavior modification techniques from their camp-trained children. Possibilities for training persons other than parents were also discussed by Blackmore, Rich, Means, and Nally (1976), Miller, Lies, Petersen, and Feallock (1976), and Rafael (1972).

ADVICE TO PARENT TRAINERS: PROCEED WITH CAUTION

It should be understood at the outset that those who use behavior modification techniques with parents should be knowledgeable about the principles underlying these procedures. To put it the other way around, those who are not skilled users of the principles and procedures of behavior modification, or are not comfortable with the process, should not use it.

Counselors also should consider carefully the ethical and practical implications of using behavior modification techniques with parents. As Wikler et al. (1976) noted, these techniques are used to manage or control the behavior of others, and such control can be practised with benevolence or with malice. Furthermore, although parents can be trained to use an almost endless number of behaviors, they should be trained to use those having the most long-term benefits. Parents have child-rearing as their primary task and they want to do a good job of it. They want to provide for their children's long-term good. It is likely that they will be enthusiastic about learning behaviors that they recognize as helping them to be better parents. Other tasks may seem to them to be nonessential or busywork. Proposed training tasks should be assessed with respect to how they meet *parental* objectives. In fact, careful selection of behaviors to be modified seems to this writer to be the most crucial part of parent training. Through discussion with the parent, a counselor can be relatively sure about which new behaviors will be useful.

Having carefully assessed the training task and explained the usefulness of the behavior to be acquired, the counselor should remember that behavior modification principles are the same for parents as for any other population. First, the total task must be simplified or separated into segments so that success is achievable. It is also wise to ask the parent to practice any new behavior only for short periods of time each day, and to enlist the parent's help in determining when these times should be. The following experience taught me that to ask a person to use a new behavior for unspecified periods of time is to invite failure.

A mother whose 5-year-old boy, Steve, avoided eye contact with her when they were conversing said she thought it would be easier for her to understand Steve if he looked at her. She agreed to try for 1 week a program that involved withholding her answer to his questions unless he looked at her. She would reinforce his eye contact by conversing with him. The condition of using this behavior only during face-to-face conversation was established in order to allow conversation to take place when eye contact was impossible, as when mother and son were in different rooms.

After a week of trying to carry out this procedure, the mother reported back, disappointed and discouraged. She realized that she had been too zealous in applying her new program. She had practically extinguished her son's attempts to converse with her by insisting that *every* time he spoke he should look at her. The program had to be modified to permit the mother to use her own good judgment about when to withhold conversation. The program was also limited to reinforcing eye contact for certain short specified periods each day. She chose to carry out the program at dinnertime and at bedtime, two situations in which Steve usually had been talkative. After a week on the more specific and limited program, this mother reported her delight that her own more consistent behavior was accompanied by a great increase in Steve's eye contact.

The woman did not return until Steve was seen again in about a year, at which time she talked about Steve's former problem. The mother laughed and said, "Oh yea, I remember how hard I worked not to be angry when he wouldn't look at me. But just keep cool and answer whenever he did give me a glance. But, you know, it's hard for me to realize what a real problem that was; we talk these days like two old cronies."

In any behavior modification program, successful performance should be reinforced. Parents also need reinforcement while they are learning. Their ultimate reward will of course be the desired changes in their children's performance, but it is the counselor's task to reinforce parental learning by rewarding their successes on the way to that goal. Positive reinforcement, or reward, is desirable because reward leads to more rapid and lasting changes than does punishment. Some type of social reinforcement is usually appropriate with parents. Exclamations such as, "That's right," "Good," "Fine," or "OK!" can be used for performance that approximates success. Trainers should be careful to use praise appropriately. People know when they have not made the requested response. Although people like being told when they have done well, they do not appreciate being told they have succeeded when they know they have not. Some parents will respond better to one type of reinforcer, and other parents to another type. As the counselor gets to know parents better, reinforcement can be more individualized.

Demonstration of the task to be learned is useful. First, it gives the parent a model to emulate. In addition, it is a test of the task's complexity. If the task is too difficult to demonstrate, it is probably too difficult for a parent to perform successfully.

Observation of another person performing a task seems to maximize initial learning for some parents, whereas others seem to prefer to start by trying to do it themselves. Some parents seem to learn best by practicing on a child other than their own before undertaking to modify their own children's behavior. Again, as counselors listen to parents' ideas and feelings, they can individualize the training program. Roleplaying can be used both for demonstration and for observation. An example illustrates how roleplaying was used by a group of mothers.

Mothers of six children in a preschool class were requested

to spend one morning per week working in the classroom. All said they wanted to participate but were afraid their children would misbehave or perform poorly while they were in the room. In further discussion, several mothers acknowledged their fear that *they* would perform poorly in the classroom; one woman said, "I'm scared to death that Sherri will clam up and I'll look like a fool nagging her to talk to the teachers when she's been talking to them for 2 weeks already. And if I really get mad at her I'll be so mortified!"

The counselor suggested that if each mother who was to work in the classroom during the following week would talk about the worst thing that could happen to her there, the group could help her practice ways of coping with these events should they occur. Following each woman's delineation of her potential task, the group engaged in roleplaying these situations, with the rest of the mothers taking the roles of children.

In the counseling session the following week, the first group of women reported their experiences. Each said she felt that she had accomplished what she had set out to do. Those mothers who were to assist during the following week then enacted the possibilities they dreaded most while the rest of the group played the roles of children.

The following two counseling sessions were devoted to parental reports about their classroom performance and additional role playing of various behavioral choices that they could make under classroom conditions.

The above example illustrates that parent training can be conducted in multiperson groups. All parents in the group need not be working on the same task. The essential conditions for training parents in larger groups are that all must wish to change a behavior, and that all must be willing to identify it in the presence of other parents and to practice or discuss alternatives with others.

The last example is also intended to highlight the need for follow-up to assess how a parent is carrying out a given program. Training programs can need modification in light of parental application. This necessitates spending time on parental reporting and discussion.

There are still many unanswered questions about all aspects of parent counseling, including parent training. For example, learning cannot be hurried and each parent will learn at his own rate. Consequently, adequate parent training has to be highly individualized. Falck (1976) noted that a large number of variables must be considered if adequate training programs are to be provided. Falck also discussed the possibility that the most effective parent training may be that done by counselors who go into the homes of those with handicapped children.

SUMMARY

Parents can be taught a large repertoire of behaviors. Most commonly, parents are taught methods for dealing with behaviors exhibited by their children. When properly done, such behavior modification programs can be useful to parents. In training, counselors continue to listen to parents and to use discussion and role-playing. Counselors who are successful in training parents are probably those who perform this function in conjunction with all the other functions previously discussed.

STUDY GUIDES FOR CHAPTER 11

Additional Readings

Bush, A., & Bonachea, M. Parental involvement in language development: The PAL program. *Language Speech and Hearing Services in Schools,* 1973, *4:* 82–85.

Green, D., Budd, K., Johnson, M., Lang, S., Pinkston, E., & Rudd, S. Training parents to modify problem child behaviors. In E. Mash, L. Handy & L. Hamerlynck, Eds.), *Behavior modification approaches to parenting.* New York: Brunner/Mazel, 1976, chap. 1.

Madsden, C., & Madsden, C. *Parents/children/discipline: A positive approach.* Boston: Allyn and Bacon, 1972, chaps. 5 and 6.

Simmons-Martin, A. A demonstration home approach with hearing impaired children. In E. Webster (Ed.), *Professional approaches with parents of handicapped children.* Springfield: Charles C. Thomas, 1976, chap. 4.

Practice Exercises

1. Identify one of the behaviors that you use consistently and that you
    would like to change. Be sure that this behavior is something that is
    fairly easy to change, such as a tendency not to awaken when the alarm
    rings, to be late for appointments, or to forget appointments or assign-
    ments. Analyze the various components of the total behavior and find a
    subpart—a target behavior—that could be modified easily. Plan a pro-
    gram of practicing a new component in place of the old one. Be sure to
    reward your successful performance. Continue this practice until you
    have successfully changed your unwanted behavior.
2. Imagine that a parent has identified a behavior that he wishes to change.
    Follow the process of selecting a target behavior to be modified that you
    followed in the previous exercise. Plan the program for changing the
    target. Also plan the way that you could explain the program to the
    father.
3. Work with one parent. Follow all the steps you have followed in the
    first two exercises. Add the actual explanation of the program, observa-
    tion and demonstration where appropriate, and follow-up on the par-
    ent's successful performance.

Epilogue

The foregoing are principles and procedures that I believe are important in parent counseling, and I would like to close this book as it began: with a statement about my faith in the worth of each person and each moment. I believe that each person who can read this book is also capable of shaping his own private world of thoughts, attitudes, and emotions. Thus each is capable of communicating more constructively and thereby of respecting and helping other people, such as parents of children with disability. It is not easy to disclose the many aspects of self to oneself, to understand them, and to communicate as oneself. Others have phrased my thoughts about this better than I can; Benjamin (1974) spoke of the task.

It is my conviction that we can change our behavior in the direction of our philosophy. In other words, we can change toward the self we wish to become. However, change involves arduous work, of the kind no one can perform for us. A pertinent book may aid us; so may a perceptive supervisor, notes, tapes, role-playing, and frank discussions with colleagues. Ultimately, change involves never-ending work that each one of us must perform within himself. (p. 155)

Parent counseling involves the continuous making of decisions and choices. We can decide a great deal of what we think about

ourselves, about parents, and about our time together. Freeman
spoke of the potential outcomes of our choices:

> Sometimes when I look at storms,
> I see a rainbow.
> Oh, then I stop and point and cry out, "Look!"
> Some say, "See that silly optimist,
> when he ought to be minding the storm,
> he's staring at rainbows!"
> But I have noticed how,
> after I point the rainbow out,
> often they stop, too,
> and point it out to others passing by.
>
> (Freeman, 1975, *Rainbows*)

Appendix A

Answers to Practice Exercise 2, page 21.

a.	D	g.	E
b.	I	h.	I
c.	D	i.	E
d.	E	j.	E
e.	E	k.	D
f.	D	l.	I

Appendix B

Classification of Questions on pages 103 and 104.

a.	C	g.	OEG
b.	C	h.	C
c.	OET	i.	OET
d.	OET	j.	OET
e.	OET	k.	C
f.	OET	l.	OEG

References

American heritage dictionary of the English language. Boston: American Heritage and Houghton-Mifflin, 1969.

Argyle, M. The syntaxes of bodily communication. In J. Benthall & T. Polhemus (Eds.), *The body as a medium of expression.* New York: E. P. Dutton, 1975.

Backus, O. Group structure in speech therapy. In L. Travis (Ed.), *Handbook of speech pathology.* New York: Appleton, 1957.

Badger, E. D. A mothers' training program—a sequel article. *Children Today,* 1972, *36,* 7–11.

Barnlund, D. Toward a meaning-centered philosophy of communication. In K. Griffin & B. Patton (Eds.), *Basic readings in interpersonal communication.* New York: Harper & Row, 1971.

Barsch, R. *The parent of the handicapped child.* Springfield: Charles C. Thomas, 1968.

Barsch, R. *Counseling with parents of emotionally disturbed children.* Springfield: Charles C. Thomas, 1970.

Barsch, R. *Counseling with parents of the mentally retarded.* Springfield: Charles C. Thomas, 1970.

Bates, M., & Johnson, C. *Group leadership: A manual for group counseling leaders.* Denver: Love, 1972.

Benjamin, A. *The helping interview.* Boston: Houghton-Mifflin, 1974.

Bice, H. *Group counseling with mothers of the cerebral palsied.* Chicago: National Society for Crippled Children and Adults, 1952.

Bissell, N. Communicating with parents of exceptional children. In E. Webster (Ed.), *Professional approaches with parents of handicapped children.* Springfield: Charles C. Thomas, 1976.

Blackmore, M., Rich, N., Means, Z., & Nally, M. Summer therapeutic environment program—STEP: A hospital alternative for children. In E. Mash, L. Handy, & L. Hamerlynck (Eds.), *Behavior modification approaches to parenting.* New York: Brunner/Mazel, 1976.

Brutten, M., Richardson, S., & Mangel, C. *Something's wrong with my child.* New York: Harcourt, Brace, Jovanovich, 1973.

Buber, M. *I and thou* (2nd ed., R. Smith, Trans.). New York: Charles Scribner's Sons, 1958.

Buscaglia, L. *The disabled and their parents: A counseling challenge.* Thorofore, New Jersey: Charles B. Slack, 1975.

Bush, C., & Bonachea, M. Parental involvement in language development: The PAL program. *Language Speech and Hearing Services in Schools.* 82–85, 1973, 4.

Carpenter, R., & Augustine, L. A pilot training program for parent-clinicians. *Journal of Speech and Hearing Disorders.* 1973, *38*, 48–58.

Carrier, J. A program of articulation therapy administered by mothers. *Journal of Speech and Hearing Disorders.* 1970, *35*, 344–353.

Cole, B. An analysis of clinician question forms and the type of parental responses elicited by these forms. Unpublished study, Memphis State University, 1975.

Corsini, R. *Roleplaying in psychotherapy: A manual.* Chicago: Aldine, 1966.

Corsini, R., Shaw, M., & Blake, R. *Roleplaying in business and industry.* New York: The Free Press, 1961.

Doernberg, N., Bernard, M., & Lenz, C. Psychoeducational treatment for parents of autistic children. In E. Webster (Ed.), *Professional approaches with parents of handicapped children.* Springfield: Charles C. Thomas, 1976.

Doernberg, N., Rosen, B., & Walker, T. *A home training program for young mentally ill children.* New York: League School for Seriously Disturbed Children, 1968.

Exceptional Parent. J. Klebanoff (Ed.) Boston: Psy-Ed. Corp.

Falck, V. Issues in planning future programs for parents of handicapped children. In E. Webster (Ed.), *Professional approaches with parents of handicapped children.* Springfield: Charles C. Thomas, 1976.

Fraiberg, S., Smith, M., & Adelson, E. An educational program for blind infants. *Journal of Special Education,* 1969, *3,* 121–139.

Fromm, E. *Escape from freedom.* New York: Holt, 1947.

Fudala, J. Using parents in public school speech therapy. *Language Speech and Hearing Services in Schools.* 1973, *4,* 91–94.

Garrett, A. *Interviewing: Its principles and methods.* New York, Family Service Association of America, 1942.

Gibb, J. Defensive communication. In K. Giffin & B. Patton (Eds.), *Basic readings in interpersonal communication.* New York: Harper & Row, 1971.

Ginott, H. *Between parent and child.* New York: Macmillan, 1965.

Goldstein, S., & Lanyon, R. Parent clinicians in the language training of an autistic child. *Journal Speech and Hearing Disorders,* 1971, *36,* 552–560.

Gordon, T. Group-centered leadership and administration. In C. Rogers (Ed.), *Client-centered therapy.* (paperback ed.). Boston: Houghton-Mifflin, 1965.

Gordon, T. *Parent effectiveness training.* New York: Wyden, 1970.

Group for the Advancement of Psychiatry. *The joys and sorrows of parenthood.* New York: Charles Scribner's Sons, 1973.

Heisler, V. *A handicapped child in the family: A guide for parents.* New York: Grune & Stratton, 1972.

Horton, K. B. Home demonstration teaching for parents of very young deaf children. *Volta Review,* 1968, *104,* 97–101.

Howe, R. *Man's need and God's action.* Greenwich, Connecticut: Seabury Press, 1953.

Hunter, M., & Shucman, H. *Early identification and treatment of the infant retardate and his family.* New York: The Shield Institute for Retarded Children, 1967.

Johnson, C., & Katz, R. Using parents as change agents for their children: A review. *Journal of Child Psychology and Psychiatry.* 1973, *14,* 181–200.

Johnson, D. *Reaching out: Interpersonal effectiveness and self-actualization.* Englewood Cliffs, New Jersey: Prentice Hall, 1972.

Johnson, J., Devitt, M., & Bueno, L. *Child management—A self-*

instructional approach. Memphis, Northeast Community Mental Health Center, 1974.

Keyes, K. S. *How to improve your thinking ability.* New York: McGraw-Hill, 1963.

Leigh, J. What we know about counseling the disabled and their parents—A review of the literature. In L. Buscaglia (Ed.), *The disabled and their parents: A counseling challenge.* Thorofare, New Jersey: Charles B. Slack, 1975.

Lowell, E. Parental skills and attitudes, including home training. In *The young deaf child: Identification and management. Acta Otolaryngologica,* Supplement No. 206, 1965.

Madsden, C., & Madsden, C. *Parents/children/discipline.* Boston: Allyn and Bacon, 1972.

Marshall, B. An analysis of clinician questions and length of parental responses in parent counseling interviews. Unpublished study, Memphis State University, 1975.

Mash, E. J., Hamerlynck, L. A., & Handy, L. C. (Eds.). *Behavior modification and families.* New York: Brunner/Mazel, 1976.

Mash, E., Handy, L., and Hamerlynck, L. *Behavior modification approaches to parenting.* New York: Brunner/Mazel, 1976.

McDonald, E. T. *Understand those feelings.* Pittsburgh: Stanwix, 1962.

McWilliams, B. Various aspects of parent counseling. In E. Webster (Ed.), *Professional approaches with parents of handicapped children.* Springfield: Charles C. Thomas, 1976.

Mehrabian, A. Significance of posture and position in the communication of attitude and status relationships. *Psychological Bulletin.* 1969, *71,* 359–372.

Mehrabian, A. Some subtleties of communication. *Language Speech and Hearing Services in Schools.* 1972, *3,* 62–67.

Miller, K., Lies, A., Petersen, D., & Feallock, R. The positive community: A strategy for applying behavioral engineering to the redesign of family and community. In E. Mash, L. Hamerlynck, & L. Handy (Eds.), *Behavior modification and families.* New York: Brunner/Mazel, 1976.

Mullahy, P. (Ed.). *The contributions of Harry Stack Sullivan.* New York: Science House, 1952.

Murphy, A. Parent counseling and exceptionality: From creative insecurity to increased humanness. In E. Webster (Ed.), *Professional approaches with parents of handicapped children.* Springfield: Charles C. Thomas, 1976.

Patton, B., & Giffin, K. *Interpersonal communication: Basic text and readings.* New York: Harper & Row, 1974.

Purtile, R. *Essays for professional helpers.* Thorofare, New Jersey: Charles B. Slack, 1975.

Rafael, B. *The summer family conference of the early education program.* New York: United Cerebral Palsy of New York, 1972.

Raymond M., Slaby, A., & Lieb, J. *The healing alliance.* New York: W. W. Norton, 1975.

Richardson, S., Dohrenwend, B., & Klein D. *Interviewing: Its forms and functions.* New York: Basic Books, 1965.

Rogers, C. *Client-centered therapy.* Boston: Houghton-Mifflin, 1951.

Rogers, C. *Client-centered therapy* (paperback ed.). Boston: Houghton-Mifflin, 1965.

Satir, V. *Conjoint family therapy.* Palo Alto: Science and Behavior Books, 1967.

Shelton, M. Areas of parental concern about retarded children. *Mental Retardation,* 1972, *2,* 38–41.

Shontz, F. Reactions to crisis. *The Volta Review,* 1965, *67,* 364–370.

Simmons-Martin, A. A demonstration home approach with hearing impaired children. In E. Webster (Ed.), *Professional approaches with parents of handicapped children.* Springfield: Charles C. Thomas, 1976.

Slater, B. Involvement in perceptual training at the kindergarten level. *Academic Therapy,* 1971, *7,* 149–154.

Sommers, R. Factors in the effectiveness of mothers trained to aid in speech correction. *Journal of Speech and Hearing Disorders,* 1962, *27,* 178–187.

Sommers, R., Furlong, A., Rhodes, R., Fichter, G., Bowser, D., Copetas, F., & Saunders, L. Effects of maternal attitudes upon improvement in articulation when mothers are trained to assist in speech correction. *Journal of Speech and Hearing Disorders,* 1964, *29,* 126–132.

Sommers, R., Shilling, S., Paul, C., Copetas, F., Bowser, D., & McClintock. Training parents of children with functional misarticulations. *Journal of Speech and Hearing Research,* 1959, *3,* 258–265.

Stent, S. Cellular communication. *Scientific American.* 1972, *227:* 43–51.

Stewart, J. *Counseling parents of exceptional children.* New York: MSS Publishing Co., 1974.

Strahan, C., & Zytowski, D. Impact of visual, vocal, and lexical cues on judgments of counselor qualities. *Journal of Counseling Psychology.* 1976, *23,* 387–393.

Taylor, F. Project cope. In E. Webster (Ed.), *Professional approaches with parents of handicapped children.* Springfield: Charles C. Thomas, 1976.

Todd, M., & Gottlieb, M. Interdisciplinary counseling in a medical setting. In E. Webster (Ed.), *Professional approaches with parents of handicapped children.* Springfield: Charles C. Thomas, 1976.

Veenstra, M. Behavior modification in the home with the mother as the experimenter: The effect of differential reinforcement on sibling negative response states. *Child Development,* 1971, *42,* 2079–2083.

Webster, E. Parent counseling by speech pathologists and audiologists. *Journal of Speech and Hearing Disorders,* 1966, *31,* 331–340.

Webster, E. Procedures for group parent counseling in speech pathology and audiology. *Journal of Speech and Hearing Disorders.* 1968, *33,* 127–131.

Webster, E. Parents of children with communication disorders. In A. Weston (Ed.), *Communicative disorders: An appraisal.* Springfield: Charles C. Thomas, 1972.

Webster, E. Studies involving parents of children with communication handicaps. *Acta Symbolica,* 1974, *5,* 25–38.

Webster, E. Counseling with parents of handicapped children. *Communicative Disorders: An Audio Journal for Continuing Education.* 1976, *1.*

Weiner, F. *Help for the handicapped child.* New York: McGraw-Hill, 1973.

Wikler, L., Savino, R., & Kyle, J. *Behavior modification parent groups: A training manual for professionals.* Thorofare, New Jersey: Charles B. Slack, 1976.

Wing, L. *Autistic children: A guide for parents.* New York: Brunner/Mazel, 1972.

Wolpe, Z. Play therapy, psychodrama, and parent counseling. In L. Travis (Ed.), *Handbook of speech pathology.* New York: Appleton, 1957.

Wyatt, G. *Language learning and communication disorders in children.* New York: The Free Press, 1969.

Wyatt, G. Parents and siblings as co-therapists. In E. Webster (Ed.), *Professional approaches with parents of handicapped children.* Springfield: Charles C. Thomas, 1976.

INDEX

a
b
c
d
7 e
8 f
9 g
0 h
1 i
8 2 j